VOCABULARY AND MORE

Level 3
Lessons 1-30

System Designer
Philip J. Solimene

Editor
Dorothy M. Bogart

Consultant
Douglas P. Barnard, Ed.D.
Director of Reading and Language Arts
Mesa (Arizona) Public Schools

EDCON

Oakdale, New York

Pronunciation key and dictionary entries are from THORNDIKE-BARNHART JUNIOR DICTIONARY
by E. L. Thorndike and Clarence L. Barnhart. Copyright © 1968 by Scott, Foresman and Company.
Reprinted by permission of the publisher.

Printed in U.S.A.
ISBN 0-931 334-98-5

CONTENTS

SEQUENCE

INTRODUCTION

What do you do when you see a word you do not know? Do you use a dictionary to learn its meaning, do you look at the parts of the word to find a "root" word, or do you try to understand the word's meaning from its context?

New words can be learned in different ways. One good way to understand the meaning of a word is to understand what it means in the sentence or paragraph where it is used. To do this, you must understand the meaning of the sentence or paragraph you are reading.

However, understanding a word in context will not always teach you all you should know about the word. A dictionary will be needed for you to learn how to pronounce the word and to learn the word's meaning or meanings.

This book will help you to:

1. Learn the use of context clues
2. Learn the use of a dictionary
3. Learn the use of different forms of words

THE WAY TO USE THIS BOOK

First, write your name on the back cover.

Next, Look at the CONTENTS page (page iii). The large black type will show you the four main parts of the book: SEQUENCE C-1 through SEQUENCE C-30, EXERCISE G, ANSWER KEY, and PROGRESS CHART.

Then, turn to SEQUENCE C-1. Look at the four pages that make up SEQUENCE C-1. Every sequence in the book is similar. Every sequence has seven sections. Sections A through F follow one another within each sequence. Section G appears toward the back of the book after all thirty sequences. Use the CONTENTS page to locate it.

The sections are:

A   Learning the Words

B   Using Context Clues

C   Checking the Meaning

D   Completing the Sentences

E   Using the Skill

F   Supplementary Writing Exercise

G   Sentences for Spelling Exercise

Instructions for each of these sections are on the next page.

Also, your teacher will provide instruction in rules for recognizing and spelling different forms of words.

A   LEARNING THE WORDS

1. Read the sentence. Think of a word that might belong in the blank. Your teacher may ask what word you chose. You may be asked why you chose that word.
2. Write the correct word in the blank space of the sentence.
3. Write the word carefully because it is a word that you are to study.

B   USING CONTEXT CLUES

1. At the top of the page are words as they appear in a dictionary. Read the words and their meanings. All the words will be used in some of the exercises. If you have trouble pronouncing a word, use the Pronunciation Key on the inside of the back cover of the book.
2. Follow the instructions for the exercise. When you have completed the exercise, check your answers with the Answer Key.

C   CHECKING THE MEANING

Follow the instructions for the exercise. When you have completed the exercise, check your answers with the Answer Key.

D   COMPLETING THE SENTENCES

Follow the instructions for the exercise. When you have completed the exercise, check your answers with the Answer Key. Enter your score on the Progress Chart.

E   USING THE SKILL

Follow the instructions for the exercise. When you have completed the exercise, check your answers with the Answer Key. Enter your score on the Progress Chart.

F	SUPPLEMENTARY WRITING EXERCISE

Follow the instructions for the exercise. There is no Answer Key for this exercise. Your teacher will check your work.

G	SENTENCES FOR SPELLING EXERCISE

1. Each sentence in this exercise contains one of your new words. The new words are underlined.

2. Two or three days after you have completed the four pages of exercises for one sequence, your teacher may want to know how well you have learned the new words. The teacher may pronounce the new word, then read the sentence that uses the word, and then pronounce the word again.

3. You are to write the word on your Spelling Exercise pad. Enter your score on the Progress Chart. Then correct any mistakes you made.

4. You might be asked to use the sentences in this exercise to give a spelling test to someone else.

A   LEARNING THE WORDS

Look at the words in the column at the right. Choose the correct word and write it in the blank to best complete the sentence.

Check and Write

1. Walter is strong enough to _____ a nail.

2. The cows will eat the _____ of hay.

3. Those large birds are _____ .

4. The _____ in my garden have many colors.

5. In fall, squirrels _____ nuts to eat in winter.

6. One of my hand _____ looks like a monkey.

7. The _____ of some plants can make people well.

8. The branch _____ and fell from the tree.

9. Mrs. Brown's _____ is eight years old.

10. Those glass _____ are very beautiful.

11. Ann likes to sleep in a room with open _____ .

12. Our house is near that _____ in the road.

13. Mr. Smith's _____ swims well.

14. The branch _____ when I stood on it.

15. The sign said, "Do not pick the _____ ."

16. The _____ of trees are deep in the ground.

17. Sue's _____ are too big for my hands.

18. Most _____ fly high and fast.

19. We will _____ at Peter's home tonight.

20. Pile the papers into a _____ .

bend	boil	divide
blanket	bundle	drawer
dreams	eagles	elves
flowers	fellows	handles
pitch	gather	guide
nickels	puppets	socks
sting	robe	root
skipped	snapped	swallowed
sandwich	son	whip
trousers	tubes	windows
sheets	windows	fans
cloud	blade	bend
son	beast	snake
flapped	trapped	snapped
flowers	forest	needles
stumps	roots	ribs
aprons	furs	puppets
eagles	buffalos	giants
glitter	gather	matter
bundle	base	chain

1

bend (bend), 1. a curve or turn; a part that is not straight: *There is a sharp bend in the road here.* 2. to curve; make crooked; be crooked; force out of a straight line: *He bent the iron bar as if it had been made of rubber. The branch began to bend as I climbed along it.* 3. move or turn in a new direction: *He bends his steps toward home now.* 4. to bow; to stoop: *She bent to the ground and picked up a stone.* 5. submit: *I bent to his will.* 6. force to submit. *n., v.,* **bent** or **bend ed, bend ing.**

bun dle (bun'dl) 1. number of things tied together or wrapped together. 2. parcel; package. 3. tie together; make up into a bundle. 4. to wrap. 5. send or go in a hurry. *n., v.* **bun dled, bun dling.**

gath er (gaTH'ə r), 1. collect; bring into one place: *He gathered his books and papers and started to work.* 2. come together: *a crowd gathered at the scene of the accident.* 3. pick; glean or pluck: *The farmers gathered their crops.* 4. put together in the mind: *I gathered from his words that he was really much upset.* 5. pull together in folds: *The dressmaker gathers a skirt at the top.* 6. one of the little folds between the stiches when cloth is gathered. 7. draw together: *The sore gathered to a head. v., n.*

root¹ (rüt), 1. the part of a plant that grows down into the soil, holds it in place, and feeds it. 2. any underground part of a plant. 3. something like a root in shape, position, use, etc.: *the root of a tooth, the roots of the hair.* 4. a part from which other things grow and develop; a cause; source: *The love of money is the root of all evil.* 5. become fixed in the ground; send out roots and begin to grow: *Some plants root more quickly than others.* 6. fix firmly: *He was rooted to*

the spot by surprise. 7. pull, tear, or dig (up, out, etc.) by the roots; get completely rid of. 8. a term used in mathematics. 2 is the square root of 4, and the cube root of 8. In the equation $x^2 + 2x-3=0$, 1 and -3 are the roots. 9. word from which others are derived. *Room* is the root of *roominess, roomer, roommate,* and *roomy.* 10. **Take root** means (1) send out roots and begin to grow. (2) become firmly fixed. *n., v.*

root² (rüt), 1. dig with the snout: *The pigs rooted up the garden.* 2. cheer. *Slang. v.*

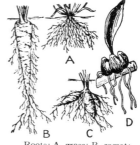

Roots: A, grass; B, carrot; C, sweet potato; D, orchid.

snap (snap), 1. make a sudden, quick bite or snatch; seize suddenly: *The dog snapped at the child's hand. The dog snapped up the meat. Jean snapped at the chance to go to college.* 2. a quick, sudden bite or snatch: *The dog made a snap at a fly.* 3. move quickly and sharply: *The soldiers snapped to attention.* 4. speak quickly and sharply: *"Silence!" snapped the captain.* 5. make or cause to make a sudden, sharp sound: *This wood snaps as it burns.* 6. a quick, sharp sound: *The box shut with a snap.* 7. break suddenly: *The violin string snapped.* 8. sudden breaking: *One snap made the knife useless.* 9. a quick, sharp way: *She moves with snap and energy.* 10. short spell of weather: *a cold snap.* 11. fastener; a clasp: *One of the snaps of your dress is unfastened.* 12. a thin crisp cooky: *a gingersnap.* 13. made or done suddenly: *A snap judgment is likely to be wrong.* 14. take a snapshot of. 15. **Not a snap** means not at all. 16. **Snap out of it** means change one's attitude or habit suddenly. *Slang. v.,* **snapped, snap ping,** *n., adj.*

B   USING CONTEXT CLUES

Place an X in front of each correct answer. The word may be used correctly in one or both of the sentences.

1. Which of the following sentences uses the underlined word correctly?
   _____ a. You must train your puppy to <u>bend</u> to your will.
   _____ b. The road <u>bends</u> to the right and then to the left.

2. A word that means about the same as <u>gather</u> is
   _____ a. pick.
   _____ b. bring.

3. Which of the following sentences uses the underlined word correctly?
   _____ a. The door <u>snapped</u> shut and I was locked out.
   _____ b. He <u>snapped</u> the button on his hat.

4. Which of the following sentences uses the underlined word correctly?
   _____ a. The <u>root</u> of Lou's trouble is the food he eats.
   _____ b. It took me three weeks to <u>root</u> this plant.

5. If Marcia got a <u>bundle</u> in the mail, she got
   _____ a.   a baby.
   _____ b.   a package.

Check your answers with the key on page 137.

C CHECKING THE MEANING

Read the words in the boxes. Choose the word that best completes the sentence under them. Write that word on the line. Then complete the next sentence by placing an X in front of the correct answer.

1. | bundle | | bundled |

   Joan _____ her baby and took him out to play in the snow.
   The word you wrote means
   ____ a. Joan put the baby in a box.
   ____ b. Joan tied up the baby.
   ____ c. Joan dressed the baby warmly.

2. | gather | | gathers |

   I _____ from what Steve said that he is not going to Beth's party.
   The word you wrote means
   ____ a. to think.
   ____ b. to come together.
   ____ c. to pick.

3. | rooted | | rooting |

   Which basketball team are you _____ for?
   The word you wrote means
   ____ a. hoping will win.
   ____ b. digging up the ground.
   ____ c. growing big and tall.

4. | snapped | | snapping |

   Stan _____ up the ball and threw it to Butch.
   The word you wrote means
   ____ a. Stan threw the ball suddenly.
   ____ b. Stan picked up the ball suddenly.
   ____ c. Stan dropped the ball suddenly.

5. | son | | sons |

   I just got a letter from my only _____ .
   The word you wrote means
   ____ a. girl child.
   ____ b. boy child.
   ____ c. father.

Check your answers with the key on page 137.

D   COMPLETING THE SENTENCES

Choose a word from the box that best completes each sentence. Write it on the line.

eagle	flower	puppet	root	window
or	*or*	*or*	*or*	*or*
eagles	flowers	puppets	roots	windows

1. Judy picked some _____ for her mother.

2. The _____ of those plants need more room in the ground.

3. Most children love to watch a _____ show.

4. Today I am going to wash five kitchen _____ .

5. Most _____ are about three feet from head to tail.

Check your answers with the key on page 137.

E   USING THE SKILL

Underline the word that best completes each sentence.

1. We do not watch much **television televisions** in my house.

2. Dinner will be ready in a few **minute minutes**.

3. The **wave waves** do not look so big from back here.

4. The answer to that **question questions** is in this book.

5. He makes twenty **dollar dollars** a day.

Check your answers with the key on page 137.

F   SUPPLEMENTARY WRITING EXERCISE

The ten new words that were taught in this lesson are:

| bend | bundle | eagles | flowers | gather |
| puppets | root | snapped | son | windows |

Choose any three of your new words from the box and write them in sentences.

1. _____

2. _____

3. _____

A	LEARNING THE WORDS

Look at the words in the column at the right. Choose the correct word and write it in the blank to best complete the sentence.

Check and Write

1.	The _____ around this lake are full of rocks.	brushes	beaches	scratches
2.	Cover yourself with this _____ .	blanket	package	shade
3.	Let's fill these _____ with books.	moments	axes	boxes
4.	I get up to the _____ of birds every morning.	pitch	chatter	respect
5.	The puppy _____ under the chair when it was afraid.	crept	poked	judged
6.	The _____ on the kitchen window is dirty.	puff	snap	curtain
7.	Did you _____ the show you saw last night?	enjoy	steal	trust
8.	I want to _____ the food left from dinner.	order	wreck	freeze
9.	Do you know what _____ make up the air?	riches	gases	events
10.	How did you get those _____ on your arm?	benches	churches	scratches
11.	At which of these _____ would you like to swim?	beaches	frames	jars
12.	The dog made those _____ on the back door.	benches	scratches	bushes
13.	I think I will _____ reading this book.	enjoy	amuse	except
14.	The boat _____ slowly along the water.	drank	fed	crept
15.	The baby always takes his _____ with him.	carpet	blanket	company
16.	I hear the chipmunk _____ when it is happy.	chatter	bubble	faint
17.	I want to make a _____ for that window.	blanket	cloud	curtain
18.	It is cold out, and the water in the pond will _____ .	gather	freeze	stray
19.	Some _____ can be used to warm our homes.	gases	jelly	iron
20.	Where did you put those _____ filled with paper?	axes	boxes	jewels

5

blan ket (blang'kit), **1.** a soft, heavy covering woven from wool or cotton. Blankets are used to keep people or animals warm. **2.** anything like a blanket: *A blanket of snow covered the ground.* **3.** cover with a blanket: *The snow blanketed the ground.* *n., v.*

chat ter (chat'ər), **1.** talk constantly in a quick, foolish way. **2.** quick, foolish talk. **3.** make quick indistinct sounds: *The monkey chattered in anger.* **4.** quick, indistinct sounds: *The chatter of sparrows annoyed her.* **5.** rattle together: *Cold makes your teeth chatter.* *v., n.*

creep (krēp), **1.** move slowly with the body lying close to the ground or floor; crawl: *Our baby learned to creep before it learned to walk.* **2.** move in a slow or sly way: *creep through the bushes.* **3.** move timidly: *The dog crept into the living room.* **4.** grow along the ground or over a wall by means of clinging stems: *a creeping plant. Ivy creeps.* **5.** feel as if things were creeping over the skin: *It made my flesh creep to hear her moan.* **6.** creeping; slow movement. *v.,* **crept, creep ing,** *n.*

cur tain (kėrt'n), **1.** cloth hung at windows or in doors for protection or ornament. **2.** a hanging screen which separates the stage of a theater from the part where the audience is. **3.** provide with a curtain; hide by a curtain. *n., v.*

en joy (en joi'), **1.** have or use with joy; be happy with; take pleasure in. **2.** have as an advantage or benefit: *He enjoyed good health.* **3. Enjoy oneself** means be happy; have a good time. *v.*

freeze (frēz), **1.** turn into ice; harden by cold. **2.** make very cold. **3.** become very cold. **4.** kill or injure by frost. **5.** cover or become covered with ice. **6.** clog with ice. **7.** a freezing. **8.** being frozen. **9.** make or become stiff and unfriendly. **10.** chill or be chilled with fear, etc. **11.** become motionless. *v.,* **froze, fro zen, freez ing,** *n.*

B	USING CONTEXT CLUES

Place an X in front of each correct answer. The word may be used correctly in one or both of the sentences.

1. A word that means about the same as crept is
   ___ a. moved.
   ___ b. crawled.

2. Which of the following sentences uses the underlined word correctly?
   ___ a. The snow covered the ground like a white blanket.
   ___ b. He blanketed the horse to make him run faster.

3. If you enjoyed a day in the park,
   ___ a. you wanted to do it again.
   ___ b. you liked the day and had fun.

4. Where would you find a curtain?
   ___ a. At a show
   ___ b. On the floor

5. Which of the following sentences uses the underlined word correctly?
   ___ a. Freeze when you see a strange dog running at you.
   ___ b. The sun froze the water in the pond.

Check your answers with the key on page 137.

C CHECKING THE MEANING

Read the words in the boxes. Choose the word that best completes the sentence under them. Write that word on the line. Then complete the next sentence by placing an X in front of the correct answer.

1. | scratch | scratches |

   Peter's writing looks like chicken _____.
   This sentence means
   ____ a. Peter writes nicely.
   ____ b. Peter's writing is hard to read.
   ____ c. Peter cannot write at all.

2. | creeping | creeps |

   That _____ plant has almost reached the windows of our house.
   The word you wrote means
   ____ a. the plant grows straight and tall.
   ____ b. the plant crawls along the ground.
   ____ c. the plant sticks to the walls of the house.

3. | chatter | chatters |

   Mary made me feel right at home with her friendly _____.
   The word you wrote means
   ____ a. Mary did most of the talking.
   ____ b. Mary didn't say very much.
   ____ c. Mary likes to talk.

4. | blanket | blanketing |

   A _____ of white fell from the sky last night.
   From this sentence, you know that
   ____ a. snow fell.
   ____ b. the moon was very bright.
   ____ c. an airplane blew up.

5. | freeze | froze |

   I _____ in my tracks, and the angry dog ran past.
   The word you wrote means
   ____ a. turned to ice.
   ____ b. stood still.
   ____ c. turned cold.

Check your answers with the key on page 137.

D COMPLETING THE SENTENCES

Choose a word from the box that best completes each sentence. Write it on the line.

beach	box	curtain	gas	scratch
or	*or*	*or*	*or*	*or*
beaches	boxes	curtains	gases	scratches

1. That bush made a big _____ on my leg.

2. I bought a _____ of candy for Toby.

3. These _____ are too long for the kitchen windows.

4. Let's stop and get some _____ for the car.

5. I hope to go to many _____ this summer.

Check your answers with the key on page 137.

E USING THE SKILL

Underline the word that best completes each sentence.

1. Which of these **dress dresses** should I wear tonight?

2. We are going to plant this **bush bushes** next to that tree.

3. Did you put those **glass glasses** on the table?

4. I'll give you three **guess guesses** as to who visited me today.

5. Put a **cross crosses** over the picture of the lion.

Check your answers with the key on page 137.

F SUPPLEMENTARY WRITING EXERCISE

The ten new words that were taught in this lesson are:

| beaches | blankets | boxes | chatter | crept |
| curtain | enjoy | freeze | gases | scratches |

Choose any three of your new words from the box and write them in sentences.

1. _____

2. _____

3. _____

Look at the words in the column at the right. Choose the correct word and write it in the blank to best complete the sentence.

Check and Write

1. Those _____ are the best I've ever eaten. | canaries | candies | companies

2. How many _____ will you visit on your trip? | armies | cities | studies

3. Janet's _____ has a new teacher. | class | organ | piano

4. There is a large _____ in this glass bottle. | group | island | crack

5. When the rain _____ stopped, we went outside. | often | finally | against

6. Where do you want to _____ these curtains? | hang | borrow | chop

7. Not one of the _____ in town had this book. | blueberries | butterflies | libraries

8. Have you found homes for your dog's _____? | jellies | puppies | worries

9. Sam _____ slowly to my question. | replied | wrote | remained

10. There are _____ children in this class. | narrow | thirty | twice

11. Harry _____ called me last night. | finally | indeed | instead

12. Which of these _____ would you like to live in? | plates | scenes | cities

13. Mary will be _____ years old next year. | thirsty | thirty | safely

14. Have you _____ to Tom's letter? | marched | leaned | replied

15. Don't eat any of those _____ before dinner. | butterflies | candies | insects

16. Bruce used a stone to _____ the nuts. | smooth | tumble | crack

17. Please _____ this picture over there. | hang | scare | press

18. These _____ are only five days old. | puppies | stems | oceans

19. Our _____ is going on a trip to the city. | nation | keeper | class

20. Many _____ have people who tell stories. | markets | libraries | highways

9

class (klas). 1. group of persons or things of the same kind. 2. group of pupils taught together. 3. their time of meeting. 4. rank of society: *upper class, middle class, working class.* 5. rank, grade, or quality: *fourth-class mail.* 6. high quality. *Used in common talk.* 7. put in a class; classify. *n., v.*

crack (krak), 1. a sudden, sharp noise like that made by loud thunder, by a whip, or by something breaking. 2. make or cause to make a sudden, sharp noise: *to crack a whip. The whip cracked.* 3. break with a sharp noise: *The tree cracked loudly and fell. We cracked the nuts.* 4. a hard, sharp blow. *Used in common talk.* 5. a split made by breaking without separating into parts: *There is a crack in this cup.* 6. break without separating into parts: *You have cracked the window.* 7. **Crack a joke** means tell a joke; say something funny. 8. excellent; first-rate: *a crack train. Used in common talk. n., v., adj.*

fi nal ly (fī′nl ē), 1. at the end; at last. 2. in such a way as to decide or close the question. *adv.*

hang (hang), 1. fasten or be fastened to something above: *Hang your cap on the hook. The swing hangs from a tree.* 2. fasten so as to leave swinging freely: *to hang a door on its hinges.* 3. put to death by hanging with a rope around the neck. 4. die by hanging. 5. depend. 6. droop; bend down: *She hung her head in shame.* 7. to cover or decorate with things that are fastened to something above: *The walls were hung with pictures.* 8. the way in which a thing hangs: *the hang of a skirt.* 9. meaning; way of using or doing: *I can't get the hang of this problem. Used in common talk.* 10. loiter; linger. 11. **Hang back** means be unwilling to go forward. 12. **Hang on** means (1) hold tight. (2) be unwilling to let go, stop, or leave. 13. **Hang together** means stick together; support each other. *v.,* **hung** (or, usually, **hanged** for 3 and 4), **hang ing,** *n.*

re ply (ri plī′), answer. *v.,* **re plied, re ply ing,** *n., pl.* **re plies.**

thir ty (thėr′tē), three times ten; 30. *n., pl.* **thir ties,** *adj.*

B USING CONTEXT CLUES

Place an X *in front of each correct answer. The word may be used correctly in one or both of the sentences.*

1. A word that means the same as replied is
   ____ a. answered.
   ____ b. cried.

2. If you finally got a letter from your brother, you got a letter
   ____ a. after a long time.
   ____ b. at the end of the day.

3. Which of the following sentences uses hang correctly?
   ____ a. Did you get the hang of what Mrs. Casidy said?
   ____ b. Hang on or you'll fall off the horse!

4. A word that means about the same as crack is
   ____ a. loud.
   ____ b. noise.

5. Thirty is
   ____ a. four tens.
   ____ b. a number.

Check your answers with the key on page 137.

C CHECKING THE MEANING

Read the words in the boxes. Choose the word that best completes the sentence under them. Write that word on the line. Then complete the next sentence by placing an X in front of the correct answer.

1. | class | | classes |

   Paul is in a _____ all by himself.
   This sentence tells you that
   ____ a. no one likes Paul.
   ____ b. Paul likes to be alone.
   ____ c. there are very few people like Paul.

2. | crack | | cracked |

   I helped Mother _____ the nuts for the cake.
   The word you wrote tells you that
   ____ a. I helped Mother cook the nuts.
   ____ b. I helped Mother break the nuts.
   ____ c. I helped Mother eat the nuts.

3. | hang | | hanging |

   My friends and I used to _____ around this corner.
   From this sentence, you know that
   ____ a. we used to wait for each other on that corner.
   ____ b. we used to walk to that corner and then walk home.
   ____ c. we used to stay on that corner and talk.

4. | crack | | cracked |

   Charles _____ a joke and got the party off to a good start.
   The word you wrote means
   ____ a. told.
   ____ b. heard.
   ____ c. made a break.

5. | libraries | | library |

   You can wait for Mr. Smythe in his _____.
   From this sentence, you know that
   ____ a. Mr. Smythe reads a lot.
   ____ b. Mr. Smythe has a room where he keeps all his books.
   ____ c. Mr. Smythe has a room where he sees people.

Check your answers with the key on page 137.

SEQUENCE C-3

D COMPLETING THE SENTENCES

Choose a word from the box that best completes each sentence. Write it on the line.

candy	city	class	library	puppy
or	*or*	*or*	*or*	*or*
candies	cities	classes	libraries	puppies

1. Would you like a piece of _____?

2. Gus went to the _____ to find a book about fish.

3. Sara's dog will have _____ soon.

4. How many _____ are you taking at school this year?

5. I have never lived in towns, only in _____.

Check your answers with the key on page 137.

E USING THE SKILL

Underline the word that best completes each sentence.

1. Would you like me to tell you a **stories story**?

2. See the **babies baby** fish swimming in the lake.

3. Thirty **families family** live in this apartment building.

4. We have a house way out in the **countries country**.

5. How many **pennies penny** are in a dollar?

Check your answers with the key on page 137.

F SUPPLEMENTARY WRITING EXERCISE

The ten new words that were taught in this lesson are:

candies	cities	class	crack	finally
hang	libraries	puppies	replied	thirty

Choose any three of your new words from the box and write them in sentences.

1. _____

2. _____

3. _____

A   LEARNING THE WORDS

Look at the words in the column at the right. Choose the correct word and write it in the blank to best complete the sentence.

Check and Write

1. Walking is very good for your _____.	calves	scarves	heels
2. Sit at your _____ and do your school work.	tank	mirror	desk
3. I want to hang this picture in the _____.	ocean	net	hall
4. Put these flowers in that _____ of water.	jar	pound	tube
5. Mel works at his _____ five days a week.	pillow	job	log
6. Our _____ made our necks too hot.	hooves	cheeks	scarves
7. Carol needs _____ in her room to hold her books.	thieves	leaves	shelves
8. Look both ways before you step off the _____.	sidewalk	cloth	beach
9. I am cooking a _____ dish for dinner tonight.	special	rubber	lonely
10. The _____ were caught taking the gold.	calves	thieves	snakes
11. Put these books on those _____.	ants	tools	shelves
12. The two _____ were caught by a policeman.	spiders	thieves	tribes
13. The mothers of these _____ are in the barn.	calves	hooves	shelves
14. The kitchen is at the end of the _____.	cliff	hall	event
15. Father's birthday is a very _____ day.	lazy	ugly	special
16. How long have you been working at your _____?	stream	job	meadow
17. Nancy wears _____ with all her clothes.	lumber	leaves	scarves
18. Harry's _____ is always covered with paper.	desk	rack	clip
19. There is no _____ in front of my house.	blade	sidewalk	island
20. The boy caught a fly and put it in a _____.	sleigh	tower	jar

13

calf[1] (kaf), 1. a young cow or bull. 2. a young elephant, whale, deer, etc. 3. leather made of the skin of a calf. *n., pl.* **calves.**

calf[2] (kaf), the thick, fleshy part of the back of the leg below the knee. *n., pl.* **calves.**

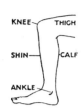

hall (hôl), 1. a way to go through a building; passageway: *A hall ran the length of the upper floor of the house.* 2. a passage or room at the entrance of a building: *Leave your umbrella in the hall.* 3. a large room for holding meetings, parties, banquets, etc.: *No hall in town was large enough for the crowd gathered to hear the famous singer.* 4. a building for public business, assemblies, etc.: *The town hall contains several offices and a big assembly room.* 5. the house of an English landowner. 6. a building of a school or college. *n.*

jar[1] (jär), deep container made of earthenware, stone, or glass, with a wide mouth. *n.*

jar[2] (jär), 1. shake; rattle: *Your heavy footsteps jar my table.* 2. make a harsh, grating noise. 3. a harsh, grating noise. 4. have a harsh, unpleasant effect on; send a shock through (one's ears, nerves, feelings, etc.): *The children's screams jar my nerves.* 5. a slight shock to the ears, nerves, feelings, etc. 6. clash; quarrel: *We did not get on well together, for our opinions always jarred.* *v.,* **jarred, jar ring,** *n.*

job (job), 1. piece of work; a definite piece of work done regularly for pay: *This carpenter has no job now.* 2. work; business; employment: *What kind of job does your father have?* 3. anything a person has to do. *n.*

scarf (skärf), 1. a long broad strip of silk, lace, etc., worn about the neck, shoulders, or head. 2. necktie with hanging ends. 3. long strip of linen, etc., used as a cover for a bureau, table, piano, etc. *n., pl.* **scarfs, scarves** (skärvz).

spe cial (spesh′əl), 1. of a particular kind; distinct from others; not general: *This desk has a special lock. Have you any special color in mind for your new coat?* 2. for a particular person, thing, purpose, etc.: *The railroad ran special trains on holidays. Send the letter by a special messenger.* 3. unusual; exceptional; more than ordinary: *Today's topic is of special interest.* 4. special train, car, bus, etc. *adj., n.*

B USING CONTEXT CLUES

Place an X in front of each correct answer. The word may be used correctly in one or both of the sentences.

1. A word that means about the same as special is
   ____ a. dollar.
   ____ b. different.

2. A hall can be a
   ____ a. building.
   ____ b. room.

3. If you have five jobs to do in a day,
   ____ a. you have five things to do.
   ____ b. you have five places where you work.

4. A scarf can be found
   ____ a. around your neck.
   ____ b. on a table.

5. Which of the following sentences uses the underlined word correctly?
   ____ a. The elephant took good care of her calf.
   ____ b. Mitchell hurt his left calf playing basketball.

Check your answers with the key on page 138.

C   CHECKING THE MEANING

Read the words in the boxes. Choose the word that best completes the sentence under them. Write that word on the line. Then complete the next sentence by placing an X in front of the correct answer.

1. | calf | | calves |

   The farmer would not sell the four young _____.
   The word you wrote means
   ____ a.   young lions.
   ____ b.   young cows.
   ____ c.   part of your leg.

2. | special | | specially |

   "This ring is very _____ to me," said Grace.
   This sentence tells you that
   ____ a.   Grace liked her ring.
   ____ b.   Grace felt the ring was important to her.
   ____ c.   Grace wanted her ring.

3. | scarf | | scarves |

   My aunt made these _____ for her children to wear next winter.
   This sentence tells you that
   ____ a.   my aunt made things to wear around the neck to keep warm.
   ____ b.   my aunt made pretty things to put on tables.
   ____ c.   my aunt made pretty things to wear around your arm.

4. | hall | | halls |

   All the rooms in my apartment open into a long _____.
   The word you wrote means
   ____ a.   a large room where you hold parties.
   ____ b.   a school building.
   ____ c.   a way to go through a building.

5. | jar | | jarred |

   Bill's jumping _____ my desk.
   The sentence means
   ____ a.   Bill made my desk move.
   ____ b.   Bill made a noise at my desk.
   ____ c.   Bill covered my desk with glasses.

Check your answers with the key on page 138.

D COMPLETING THE SENTENCES

Choose a word from the box that best completes each sentence. Write it on the line.

calf	scarf	shelf	sidewalk	thief
or	*or*	*or*	*or*	*or*
calves	scarves	shelves	sidewalks	thieves

1. You may ride your bicycle on the _____ in front of the house.

2. A _____ took things from our house last night.

3. My _____ hurt from dancing so much last night.

4. Richard made these _____ to hold our books.

5. It is cold out, so put a _____ on your head.

Check your answers with the key on page 138.

E USING THE SKILL

Underline the word that best completes each sentence.

1. My horse's **hoof hooves** are sore.

2. I will go to the party dressed as an **elf elves**.

3. Gather the **leaf leaves** and put them in this bag.

4. Bob, you can do that by **yourself yourselves**.

5. There are **wolf wolves** living in these woods.

Check your answers with the key on page 138.

F SUPPLEMENTARY WRITING EXERCISE

The ten new words that were taught in this lesson are:

| calves | desk | hall | jar | job |
| scarves | shelves | sidewalk | special | thieves |

Choose any three of your new words from the box and write them in sentences.

1. _____

2. _____

3. _____

A LEARNING THE WORDS

Look at the words in the column at the right. Choose the correct word and write it in the blank to best complete the sentence.

Check and Write

1. Let's sit on this _____ and rest.

bench   soap   page

2. Let's ride our _____ this afternoon.

worms   bicycles   tanks

3. Many _____ of that tree need to be cut.

touches   benches   branches

4. I would like another _____ to win that prize.

chance   plan   inch

5. Our football _____ works hard with the team.

group   helper   coach

6. The two _____ of this apple are the same.

leaves   halves   shelves

7. Will you _____ please find seats.

ladies   cities   candies

8. We may _____ the basketball game today.

loose   imagine   lose

9. Our football _____ plays every Saturday in the fall.

pitcher   team   company

10. Don't _____, I'll be careful.

worry   wander   stray

11. Will you _____ our team this year?

offer   coach   plan

12. Who will ride these _____ in today's race?

bicycles   groups   mice

13. I'll give you one more _____ to guess the answer.

charge   fear   chance

14. Don't _____ about Danny, he'll be all right.

growl   worry   learn

15. Nina filled the fruit _____ with ice cream.

halves   flaps   hearts

16. I sat on a park _____ and waited for Dick.

beard   drum   bench

17. Which _____ will win the race?

carrot   team   test

18. These _____ drive the school buses.

ladies   puppies   visitors

19. Why did you _____ the game?

scatter   understand   lose

20. The _____ of that tree are full of leaves.

benches   needles   branches

17

branch (branch), 1. part of a tree that grows out from the trunk; any large, woody part of a tree above the ground except the trunk. 2. a division: *a branch of a river, a branch of a family. Arithmetic is a branch of learning.* 3. put out branches; spread in branches. 4. divide: *The road branches at the bottom of the hill. n., v.*

chance (chans), 1. opportunity: *a chance to make some money.* 2. possibility; probability: *There is a chance that the sick child will get well.* 3. fate; luck. 4. a happening: *Chance led to the finding of the diamond mine.* 5. happen. 6. risk. 7. not expected; accidental: *a chance visit. n., v.,* chanced, chanc ing, *adj.*

coach (kōch), 1. a large, old-fashioned, closed carriage with seats inside. Some coaches, which carried passengers along a regular run, with stops for meals and fresh horses, often had seats on top too. 2. a passenger car of a railroad train. 3. a teacher: *the football coach.* 4. train or teach. 5. make ready for a special test. *n., v.*

Coach

lose (lüz), 1. not have any longer; have taken away from one by accident, carelessness, parting, death, etc.: *to lose a dollar, to lose one's life, to lose a limb, to lose a father, to lose a friend.* 2. fail to keep: *to lose your patience, to lose your temper.* 3. be or become worse off in money, in numbers, etc.: *The army lost heavily in yesterday's battle.* 4. become unable to find: *to lose a book.* 5. waste; spend or let go by without any result: *to lose time waiting, to lose one's trouble, to lose a chance.* 6. miss; fail to get, catch, see, or hear: *to lose a train, to lose a few words of what was said.* 7. not to win; be defeated: *to lose a bet or a game.* 8. cause one to lose: *That one act lost him his job.* 9. Some special meanings are: **be lost,** have lost one's way. **be lost in** (something), be so taken up with it that one fails to notice anything else. **lose (one's) way,** not to know any longer where one is. *v.,* lost, los ing.

team (tēm), 1. number of people working or acting together: *a football team, a debating team.* 2. two or more horses or other animals harnessed together to work. 3. join together in a team. *n., v.*

wor ry (wėr′ē), 1. feel anxious; be uneasy: *She worries about little things.* 2. bother; annoy; vex; trouble: *Don't worry your father with so many questions.* 3. care; anxiety; uneasiness; trouble. 4. seize and shake with the teeth; bite at; snap at: *The dog worried the rat. v.,* wor ried, wor ry ing, *n., pl.* wor ries.

B USING CONTEXT CLUES

Place an X in front of each correct answer. The word may be used correctly in one or both of the sentences.

1. A coach can be found
   _____ a. on a train.
   _____ b. on a road.

2. Worry could mean
   _____ a. bite at.
   _____ b. trouble.

3. Which of the following sentences uses the underlined word correctly?
   _____ a. Let's all team together and win the game.
   _____ b. I hope they don't team me up with Margo at the egg hunt.

4. Which of the following sentences uses the underlined word correctly?
   _____ a. Uncle Fred is from Father's branch of the family.
   _____ b. The building branched straight up for thirty stories.

5. A word that means about the same as lose is
   _____ a. fair.
   _____ b. miss.

Check your answers with the key on page 138.

C CHECKING THE MEANING

Read the words in the boxes. Choose the word that best completes the sentence under them. Write that word on the line. Then complete the next sentence by placing an X in front of the correct answer.

1. | worried | | worrying |

The cat _____ the mouse.
The word you wrote means
____ a. belonged to.
____ b. didn't believe.
____ c. snapped at.

2. | chance | | chanced |

Just by _____, Steve met Tom in the park.
This sentence means
____ a. Steve knew he would meet Tom.
____ b. Steve didn't know he would meet Tom.
____ c. Steve was happy to meet Tom.

3. | coach | | coaches |

Charles will _____ George for his new job.
The word you wrote means
____ a. bus.
____ b. car.
____ c. make ready.

4. | lose | | lost |

I'm sorry I'm late, but I got _____ getting here.
From this sentence, you know that
____ a. I didn't know where I was.
____ b. I could not find the house.
____ c. I spent a lot of time getting there.

5. | branch | | branches |

A large river _____ near my town.
This sentence means
____ a. the river has leaves.
____ b. the river moves around a tree.
____ c. the river sends water more than one place.

Check your answers with the key on page 138.

D COMPLETING THE SENTENCES

Choose a word from the box that best completes each sentence. Write it on the line.

bicycle	branch	half	lady	worry
or	*or*	*or*	*or*	*or*
bicycles	branches	halves	ladies	worries

1. Rudy does not have anything to _____ him.

2. The _____ of that tree are very straight.

3. Are you sure you want to eat _____ this pie?

4. We bought Vic a new _____ for his birthday.

5. That _____ has lost her gloves.

Check your answers with the key on page 138.

E USING THE SKILL

Underline the word that best completes each sentence.

1. Those **ponies pony** are very beautiful animals.

2. My Aunt Ida gave me this set of **dish dishes**.

3. Why are you always getting into **fight fights**?

4. This **scarf scarves** is much too long for me to wear.

5. Are you going to a **party parties** tomorrow night?

Check your answers with the key on page 138.

F SUPPLEMENTARY WRITING EXERCISE

The ten new words that were taught in this lesson are:

bench	bicycles	branches	chance	coach
halves	ladies	lose	team	worry

Choose any three of your new words from the box and write them in sentences.

1. _____

2. _____

3. _____

A	LEARNING THE WORDS

Look at the words in the column at the right. Choose the correct word and write it in the blank to best complete the sentence.

Check and Write

1. Joan _____ go to the party because she is sick.   can't   haven't   doesn't

2. When you eat, _____ your food well.   comb   chew   divide

3. Watch the squirrel _____ up the tree.   march   flow   dash

4. Matthew _____ remember his Uncle Joe.   doesn't   hasn't   haven't

5. The beach _____ too far from our house.   can't   shouldn't   isn't

6. Do you know what Tracy _____ when she said that?   hid   meant   taught

7. We almost always have _____ for dinner.   meat   snake   paste

8. Where will you get _____ of these old things?   ought   aim   rid

9. Milk must be kept cold so that it will not _____ .   boil   spoil   disappear

10. My dog _____ bite you; he's friendly.   wasn't   hasn't   won't

11. I never _____ for you to think that!   thought   meant   mount

12. The dog will _____ through that rope in no time.   chew   trade   squeak

13. My dog likes to _____ after birds.   dare   dash   continue

14. Why _____ you let me go out?   doesn't   isn't   won't

15. Roberta _____ know how to ride a bicycle.   hasn't   doesn't   haven't

16. I hope the rain doesn't _____ our picnic.   spoil   complete   spare

17. Lucy _____ in school today.   wouldn't   isn't   couldn't

18. Finish your _____ and then I'll give you some ice cream.   mice   oil   meat

19. How can we get _____ of those bees?   rid   thirsty   born

20. If you _____ be quiet, you'll have to leave.   shouldn't   don't   couldn't

chew (chü), 1. crush or grind with the teeth: *We chew food.* 2. a bite. *v., n.*

dash (dash), 1. throw: *We dashed water over him.* 2. rush: *They dashed by in a car.* 3. **Dash off** sometimes means do quickly. 4. small amount: *Put in just a dash of pepper.* 5. a short race: *the 100-yard dash.* 6. a mark (—) used in writing or printing. *v., n.*

mean (mēn), 1. intend; have as a purpose; have in mind: *Do you think they mean to fight us? Do you mean to use the chops for dinner? He was meant for a soldier.* **Mean well by** means have kindly feelings toward. 2. have as its thought; intend to say: *Can you make out what this sentence means?* *v.,* **meant, mean ing.**

meat (mēt), 1. animal flesh used for food. Fish and poultry are usually not called meat. 2. food: *meat and drink.* 3. part that can be eaten: *the meat of a nut.* *n.*

rid (rid), make free: *What will rid a house of rats?* **Be rid of** means to be freed from. **Get rid of** means (1) get free from: *I can't get rid of this cold.* (2) do away with. *v.,* **rid or rid ded, rid ding.**

spoil (spoil), 1. damage; injure; destroy: *He spoils a dozen pieces of paper before he writes a letter. The rain spoiled the picnic. That child is spoiled by too much attention.* 2. be damaged; become bad or unfit for use: *Fruit spoils if kept too long.* 3. things taken by force; things won: *The soldiers carried the spoils back to their own land.* *v.,* **spoiled or spoilt, spoil ing,** *n.*

B USING CONTEXT CLUES

Place an X *in front of each correct answer. The word may be used correctly in one or both of the sentences.*

1. If you dashed off a letter to your sister,
   - ___ a. you were writing it quickly.
   - ___ b. you threw away the letter.

2. Which of the following sentences uses the underlined word correctly?
   - ___ a. I'm to meat Lois at the library.
   - ___ b. The meat of this fruit is very soft.

3. Which of the following sentences uses the underlined word correctly?
   - ___ a. Alfred meant to visit us, but he didn't have the time.
   - ___ b. Harold means well, but I wish he'd stop trying to help me.

4. If you have some spoils,
   - ___ a. you have things that are no good.
   - ___ b. you have things that you took.

5. Which of the following sentences uses the underlined word correctly?
   - ___ a. We are now rid of the ants in our apartment.
   - ___ b. Will you rid a horse in the parade?

Check your answers with the key on page 138.

C CHECKING THE MEANING

Read the words in the boxes. Choose the word that best completes the sentence under them.
Write that word on the line. Then complete the next sentence by placing an X in front of the
correct answer.

1. | rid | | ridding |

   Before he was caught, the thief got _____ of the rings he took.
   From this sentence, you know that
   ____ a. the thief tried to sell the rings.
   ____ b. the thief threw away the rings.
   ____ c. the thief tried to win the rings.

2. | dash | | dashed |

   Vivian _____ down to the water and jumped in.
   In this sentence, the word you wrote means
   ____ a. rushed.
   ____ b. threw.
   ____ c. short race.

3. | means | | meant |

   Mr. Brown _____ to send Brian to a special school next year.
   The word you wrote means
   ____ a. plans.
   ____ b. believes.
   ____ c. thinks.

4. | spoil | | spoiled |

   Those fruits will _____ if this freezing rain keeps up.
   This sentence tells you that
   ____ a. the fruits will be fit.
   ____ b. the fruits will be taken.
   ____ c. the fruits will be not fit to eat.

5. | chew | | chewed |

   The squirrel held the nut in its paws and _____ it.
   The word you wrote means
   ____ a. ate.
   ____ b. bit.
   ____ c. smelled.

Check your answers with the key on page 138.

SEQUENCE C-6

D COMPLETING THE SENTENCES

Choose a word from the box that best completes each sentence. Write it on the line.

can	does	is	will	would
or	*or*	*or*	*or*	*or*
can't	doesn't	isn't	won't	wouldn't

1. There _____ seem to be any good road through that field.

2. Jack has to work late, so he _____ be late for dinner.

3. She _____ help us last week, so we didn't help her this week.

4. The children _____ get through the snow and will have to stay home today.

5. They said it would rain, but so far there _____ any.

Check your answers with the key on page 138.

E USING THE SKILL

Underline the word that best completes each sentence.

1. Larry has broken his leg and so he **could couldn't** drive.

2. I **have haven't** heard from Mark for three weeks.

3. Why **do don't** you come for dinner tomorrow?

4. Phil **was wasn't** not at home when I called.

5. If you wanted to go, why **did didn't** you say so?

Check your answers with the key on page 138.

F SUPPLEMENTARY WRITING EXERCISE

The ten new words that were taught in this lesson are:

can't	chew	dash	doesn't	isn't
meant	meat	rid	spoil	won't

Choose any three of your new words from the box and write them in sentences.

1. _____

2. _____

3. _____

Look at the words in the column at the right. Choose the correct
word and write it in the blank to best complete the sentence.

Check and Write

1. The mail _____ at ten o'clock every morning.

arrives   announces   explains

2. I hope Bonnie _____ to do well in school.

invites   continues   complains

3. I never remember the _____ I have at night.

maps   forms   dreams

4. That animal's _____ is very soft.

fur   frame   cheek

5. I want to ride my bicycle in the ten-_____ race.

carrot   fiddle   mile

6. Our teacher will be here in a _____ .

giant   moment   shake

7. No pushing is a _____ that everyone must follow.

rule   shape   robe

8. I must _____ home and take my dog for a walk.

steal   nod   rush

9. There are many cracks in the _____ by my house.

route   sidewalk   stream

10. Those lights are _____ for the racing car drivers.

signals   handles   needles

11. Philip left for work just a _____ ago.

shadow   moment   bargain

12. Tommy _____ at school at eight o'clock.

arrives   plows   awakes

13. Strong _____ were coming from the ship's radio.

scents   mirrors   signals

14. I'm in a terrible _____ to get home.

rattle   rush   force

15. Miriam just bought a beautiful _____ coat.

fierce   lead   fur

16. If this rain _____, streets will be closed.

continues   cracks   bubbles

17. The children jumped rope on the _____.

shore   nation   sidewalk

18. One _____ in this house is bedtime at seven o'clock.

root   rule   shoot

19. Mary _____ of walking on the moon.

dreams   acts   models

20. I walk a _____ to work every day.

map   nickel   mile

25

con tin ue (kən tin'ū), **1.** keep up; keep on; not stop; last; cause to last: *The rain continued all day.* **2.** maintain; retain: *Mr. Wilson was continued in office for two terms.* **3.** stay: *The children must continue at school till July. Jack continues happy.* **4.** take up; carry on: *The story will be continued next month.* **5.** put off until a later time; postpone; adjourn. *v.,* **con tin ued, con tin u ing.**

dream (drēm), **1.** something thought, felt, or seen in sleep. **2.** something as unreal as the fancies of sleep: *The boy had dreams of being a hero.* **3.** think, feel, hear, or see in sleep. **4.** form fancies; imagine: *The girl dreamed of being in the movies.* **5.** suppose in a vague way: *The day seemed so bright that we never dreamed there would be rain. n., v.,* **dreamed** or **dreamt, dream ing.**

mile (mīl), a distance equal to 5280 feet; statute mile. A nautical or geographical mile is about 6080 feet. *n.*

mo ment (mō'mənt), **1.** a very short space of time; an instant: *I started the very moment I got your message. n.*

rush (rush), **1.** move or go with speed and force: *The river rushed past.* **2.** send, push, or force with speed or haste: *Rush this order, please.* **3.** go or act with great haste: *He rushes into things without knowing anything about them.* **4.** to attack with much speed and force: *The soldiers rushed the enemy's trenches.* **5.** hurry: *What is your rush? Wait a minute. v., n., adj.*

sig nal (sig'nl), **1.** sign giving notice of something: *A red light is a signal of danger.* **2.** make a signal or signals (to): *He signaled the car to stop by raising his hand. n., v.,* **sig naled, sig nal ing,** *adj.*

B USING CONTEXT CLUES

Place an X *in front of each correct answer. The word may be used correctly in one or both of the sentences.*

1. If you rushed to get home by five o'clock,
   ____ a. you hurried.
   ____ b. you ran.

2. Which of the following sentences uses the underlined word correctly?
   ____ a. I never dreamed I would enjoy that book so much.
   ____ b. Joe's dreams are always happy.

3. If you continue reading a book,
   ____ a. you keep reading it without stopping.
   ____ b. you put off reading it until later.

4. Where would you see a signal light?
   ____ a. In the street
   ____ b. In your house

5. Which of the following sentences uses the underlined word correctly?
   ____ a. It took me a moment to walk a mile.
   ____ b. I'll be ready to leave in a moment.

Check your answers with the key on page 139.

C CHECKING THE MEANING

Read the words in the boxes. Choose the word that best completes the sentence under them.
Write that word on the line. Then complete the next sentence by placing an X in front of the
correct answer.

1. | rush | | rushed |

   The policeman _____ to the house where the thieves were.
   From this sentence, you know that
   ____ a. the policeman walked slowly and carefully towards the house.
   ____ b. the policeman hurt the thieves that were in the house.
   ____ c. the policeman ran to the house very quickly.

2. | mile | | miles |

   The dog chased the car one _____ down the road before stopping.
   From this sentence, you know that
   ____ a. the dog ran 5280 feet.
   ____ b. the dog ran 10,000 feet.
   ____ c. the dog ran 6080 feet.

3. | continue | | continues |

   I will _____ at my job until March.
   From this sentence, you know that
   ____ a. I will stay at my job until March and then leave.
   ____ b. I will leave my job now and come back in March.
   ____ c. I will stay at my job and not leave at all.

4. | dream | | dreams |

   Ricky _____ of having all the money in the world.
   The word you wrote means
   ____ a. thinks about it much of the time.
   ____ b. thinks about it only while asleep.
   ____ c. never thinks about it.

5. | moment | | moments |

   The _____ he saw the woman's face, Mr. Clark knew it was his sister.
   The word you wrote means
   ____ a. the first time.
   ____ b. the very second.
   ____ c. a minute or so.

Check your answers with the key on page 139.

D COMPLETING THE SENTENCES

Choose a word from the box that best completes each sentence. Write it on the line.

arrive	continue	dream	laugh	signal
or	*or*	*or*	*or*	*or*
arrives	continues	dreams	laughs	signals

1. People _____ many times while they are sleeping.

2. When your train _____, I will meet you.

3. People who visit _____ me with the doorbell.

4. My baby _____ every time he sees his grandfather.

5. Jeff will _____ reading his book tomorrow.

Check your answers with the key on page 139.

E USING THE SKILL

Underline the word that best completes each sentence.

1. I must **write writes** my brother a letter today.

2. Watch the children **skate skates** down the street.

3. Walter **leave leaves** the house at nine every morning.

4. I'm going to **visit visits** Vera today.

5. Look how the puppy **follow follows** Bruce everywhere he goes.

Check your answers with the key on page 139.

F SUPPLEMENTARY WRITING EXERCISE

The ten new words that were taught in this lesson are:

arrives	continues	dreams	fur	mile
moment	rule	rush	sidewalk	signals

Choose any three of your new words from the box and write them in sentences.

1. _____

2. _____

3. _____

A LEARNING THE WORDS

Look at the words in the column at the right. Choose the correct word and write it in the blank to best complete the sentence.

Check and Write

1. We have _____ had our dinner.

already   often   instead

2. We are having snow, so wear your _____.

beads   boots   jewels

3. **The painter's** _____ are hard to clean.

knives   plates   brushes

4. The boys found foxes living in a _____.

automobile   cave   pool

5. George was very _____ to go on the class trip.

eager   lonely   gentle

6. What is the _____ with Beverly?

motor   honor   matter

7. Mark _____ peanut butter with apples.

mixes   crashes   kisses

8. I still have to _____ my clothes for my trip.

dust   pack   guard

9. Many _____ were made for the missing dog.

switches   marches   searches

10. A cat always _____ before it gets up.

stretches   crashes   breathes

11. You don't seem to be _____ to visit your grandmother

built   eager   fresh

12. I have _____ read that book.

softly   usually   already

13. Harry always _____ his shoes after wearing them.

stretches   matches   dashes

14. I want to _____ these old dishes in this box.

lower   pack   rattle

15. Wendy has new _____ lined with fur.

stamps   flaps   boots

16. The thieves lived in a small mountain _____.

cave   ocean   bowl

17. I enjoy it when someone _____ my hair.

rushes   brushes   dashes

18. Rosa _____ blue with yellow to make green.

mixes   draws   matches

19. When you are sad, nothing seems to _____.

form   appear   matter

20. The bird _____ the ground, looking for food.

dusts   searches   stretches

29

brush (brush), 1. clean, rub, paint, etc., with a brush; use a brush on. 2. remove; wipe away: *The child brushed the tears from his eyes.* 3. touch lightly in passing. 4. short, brisk fight or quarrel. *n., v.*

mat ter (mat'ər), 1. importance: *Let it go since it is of no matter.* 2. be important: *Nothing seems to matter when you are very sick.* 3. affair: *business matters, a matter of life and death.* 4. Some special meanings are: **as a matter of fact,** in truth; in reality. **for that matter,** so far as that is concerned. **matter of course,** something that is to be expected. **no matter, 1.** Let it go; it isn't important. **2.** regardless of. **"What is the matter?"** means "What is wrong?" *n., v.*

mix (miks), 1. put together; stir well together: *We mix butter, sugar, milk, and flour for a cake.* 2. prepare by putting different things together: *to mix a cake.* 3. join; be mixed: *Oil and water will not mix.* 4. associate; get along together: *Katy likes people and mixes well in almost any group.* 5. **Mix up** sometimes means confuse: *I was so mixed up that I did very badly on the examination.* *v.,* **mixed** or **mixt, mix ing.**

pack (pak), 1. bundle of things wrapped up or tied together for carrying: *The soldier carried a pack on his back.* 2. put together in a bundle, box, etc.: *Pack your books in this box. Peaches are often packed in cans for the market.* 3. press or crowd closely together: *A hundred men were packed into one small room.* 4. set; lot; a number together: *a pack of thieves, a pack of nonsense, a pack of lies.* 5. a number of animals hunting together; a number of dogs kept together for hunting. 6. **Pack** (a person) **off** means send him away. **Send** (a person) **packing** means send him away in a hurry. *n., v.*

search (sėrch), 1. try to find by looking; seek; look for (something); look through; go over carefully; examine: *We searched all day for the lost kitten. The police searched the prisoner to see if he had a gun. The doctor searched the wound for the bullet.* **Search out** means to find by searching. 2. searching; examination: *John found his book after a long search.* **In search of** means trying to find; looking for. *v., n.*

stretch (strech), 1. draw out; extend: *The bird stretched its wings. The blow stretched him out on the ground.* 2. extend one's body or limbs: *John arose and stretched.* 3. reach out; hold out: *He stretched out a hand for money.* 4. draw tight; strain: *He stretched the violin string until it broke.* 5. continue over a distance; extend from one place to another; fill space; spread: *The forest stretches for miles to the westward.* 6. unbroken length; extent: *A stretch of sand hills lay between the road and the ocean.* *v., n.*

B   USING CONTEXT CLUES

Place an X in front of each correct answer. The word may be used correctly in one or both of the sentences.

1. If you sent a person underline{packing},
    _____ a.   you helped him pack his things.
    _____ b.   you sent him away in a hurry.

2. "What is the matter?" means
    _____ a.   "What is important?"
    _____ b.   "What is wrong?"

3. Which of the following sentences uses the underlined word correctly?
    _____ a.   This stretch of beach is always empty.
    _____ b.   He stretched the baby to him.

4. If I felt something brush my arm,
    _____ a.   it touched me lightly.
    _____ b.   it hit me hard.

5. If you search for something,
    _____ a.   you look for it.
    _____ b.   you find it.

Check your answers with the key on page 139.

C CHECKING THE MEANING

Read the words in the boxes. Choose the word that best completes the sentence under them. Write that word on the line. Then complete the next sentence by placing an X in front of the correct answer.

1. | brush | | brushing |

Helen had a _____ with Mary.
From this sentence, you know that
____ a. Helen cleaned Mary's hair.
____ b. Helen had a short fight with Mary.
____ c. Helen and Mary painted together.

2. | mix | | mixes |

Heidi _____ well with people.
From this sentence, you know that
____ a. Heidi gets along well with people.
____ b. Heidi knows which people will enjoy each other.
____ c. Heidi doesn't like people at all.

3. | searches | | searching |

Paulo is _____ for his brother.
The word you wrote means
____ a. looking at.
____ b. looking for.
____ c. found.

4. | packed | | packs |

Many _____ of dogs have been spotted near here.
The word you wrote means
____ a. large.
____ b. hunters.
____ c. a number of.

5. | stretched | | stretches |

The party _____ well into the early morning.
From this sentence, you know that
____ a. the party continued for a long time.
____ b. the party ended early.
____ c. the party went on longer than anyone thought.

Check your answers with the key on page 139.

D COMPLETING THE SENTENCES

Choose a word from the box that best completes each sentence. Write it on the line.

brush	mix	search	stretch	watch
or	*or*	*or*	*or*	*or*
brushes	mixes	searches	stretches	watches

1. There is a _____ of beach not too far from here.

2. The baby _____ his mother no matter where she goes.

3. The snow will _____ with rain later today.

4. I want you to _____ for that missing book.

5. Timmy _____ his sister's hair every morning.

Check your answers with the key on page 139.

E USING THE SKILL

Underline the word that best completes each sentence.

1. Every year on my birthday I make a **wish wishes**.

2. Frank wants to **teach teaches** young children.

3. Vera throws the ball and Hank **catch catches** it.

4. My father **fix fixes** everything around the house.

5. Can you **guess guesses** who called me today?

Check your answers with the key on page 139.

F SUPPLEMENTARY WRITING EXERCISE

The ten new words that were taught in this lesson are:

already	boots	brushes	cave	eager
matter	mixes	pack	searches	stretches

Choose any three of your new words from the box and write them in sentences.

1. _____

2. _____

3. _____

A   LEARNING THE WORDS

Look at the words in the column at the right. Choose the correct word and write it in the blank to best complete the sentence.

Check and Write

1. In _____, many leaves turn red and gold.   autumn   church   America

2. A policeman's job is full of _____.   smoke   direction   danger

3. Has Jack _____ when he will have his party?   decided   wired   dared

4. Sherry's life is full of fun and _____.   difference   practice   excitement

5. The policeman had his _____ in his hand.   apron   gun   heart

6. Jenny _____ that a bear was in her room.   imagined   amazed   scared

7. Orlando _____ me to his house for dinner.   served   rescued   invited

8. Pete makes _____ money than Joe.   tight   less   lower

9. Kathleen _____ her part in the play.   practiced   spared   guided

10. Mr. Lewis _____ at an empty can.   spoke   taught   shot

11. Annie _____ batting for the game on Saturday.   proved   practiced   tasted

12. Ten _____ six is four.   less   space   unless

13. I think _____ is the prettiest time of the year.   travel   blossom   autumn

14. There is _____ in playing in the streets.   escape   danger   darkness

15. The sound of a _____ broke the morning quiet.   shot   clip   tunnel

16. Pedro _____ that he was a great football player.   managed   behaved   imagined

17. Miss Turner kept her _____ in a safe place.   cellar   gun   blanket

18. Betty _____ to buy a green coat.   decided   sensed   continued

19. What _____ when all the lights went out!   calm   beauty   excitement

20. Were you _____ to Joan's party?   announced   invited   divided

33

de cide (di sīd'), **1.** settle; *Let us decide it by tossing a penny.* **2.** give judgment: *Mother decided in favor of the blue dress.* **3.** resolve; make up one's mind: *John decided to be a sailor.* *v.,* **de cid ed, de cid ing.**

gun (gun), **1.** weapon with a metal tube for shooting bullets, shot, etc. A rifle or cannon is a gun. Pistols and revolvers are called guns in ordinary talk. **2.** shooting of a gun as a signal or salute: *The President gets twenty-one guns as a salute.* **3.** shoot with a gun; hunt with a gun: *Bill went gunning for rabbits.* *n., v.,* **gunned, gun ning.**

in vite (in vīt'), **1.** ask (someone) politely to come to some place or to do something: *We invited Helen to join our club.* **2.** attract; tempt: *The calm water invited us to swim.* *v.,* **in vit ed, in vit ing.**

less (les), **1.** not so much; not so much of: *to have less rain, to put on less butter, to eat less meat.* **2.** smaller amount: *could do no less, weigh less than before, refuse to take less than $5.* **3.** with (something) taken away; without: *five less two, a coat less one sleeve.* *adj., adv., n., prep.*

prac tice (prak'tis), **1.** the skill gained by experience or exercise: *He was out of practice at batting.* **2.** do (some act) again and again to learn to do it well: *Anne practices on the piano every day.* **3.** do usually; make a custom of: *Practice what you preach.* **4.** the usual way; the custom: *It is the practice in our town to blow the whistles at noon.* **5.** do something as a habit or profession: *That young man is just beginning to practice as a lawyer.* **6.** the business of a doctor or a lawyer: *Dr. Adams sold his practice.* *n., v.,* **prac ticed, prac tic ing.**

shot (shot), **1.** act of shooting. **2.** tiny balls of lead; bullets; single ball of lead for a gun or cannon. **3.** discharge of a gun or cannon: *He heard two shots.* **4.** an attempt to hit by shooting: *That was a good shot and it hit the mark.* **5.** person who shoots: *Mr. Smith is a good shot.* **6. A long shot** is an attempt at something difficult. **7. Not by a long shot** means not at all. **8. Shot through with** means full of. *n., pl.* **shots** or for def. 2 **shot.**

B   USING CONTEXT CLUES

Place an X in front of each correct answer. The word may be used correctly in one or both of the sentences.

1. If Dr. Catalano gave up his <u>practice</u>,
   ____ a. he no longer helped sick people.
   ____ b. he didn't do what he was supposed to do.

2. Which of the following sentences uses the underlined word correctly?
   ____ a. The <u>shot</u> was heard by many people.
   ____ b. Mrs. Fredericks is a good <u>shot</u>.

3. If Christopher <u>decided</u> to be a fireman,
   ____ a. he made up his mind.
   ____ b. he wanted it very much.

4. Which of the following sentences uses the underlined word correctly?
   ____ a. The water was very <u>inviting</u>, but we did not swim.
   ____ b. Betsy was <u>invited</u> for lunch.

5. Which of the following sentences uses the underlined word correctly?
   ____ a. Mr. White went <u>gunning</u> for wild animals.
   ____ b. Martin likes to chew <u>gun</u>.

Check your answers with the key on page 139.

C CHECKING THE MEANING

Read the words in the boxes. Choose the word that best completes the sentence under them.
Write that word on the line. Then complete the next sentence by placing an X in front of the
correct answer.

1. practice   practiced

   It is the _____ in Wendy's house to eat dinner at six o'clock.
   From this sentence, you know that
   ____ a. Wendy's family sometimes eats dinner at six o'clock.
   ____ b. Wendy's family almost always eats dinner at six o'clock.
   ____ c. Wendy's family never eats dinner at six o'clock.

2. shot   shots

   Phil had three _____ out of the five he tried.
   The word you wrote means
   ____ a. noises made when a gun is fired.
   ____ b. hits made.
   ____ c. small balls fired from a gun.

3. imagine   imagined

   In her dream, Phyllis _____ she was flying an airplane.
   From this sentence, you know that
   ____ a. Phyllis can really fly an airplane.
   ____ b. Phyllis hoped she would fly an airplane some day.
   ____ c. Phyllis pictured herself flying an airplane.

4. invited   inviting

   "That cold drink looks very _____ on such a hot day," said Pete.
   From this sentence, you know that
   ____ a. Pete is hot and wants a drink.
   ____ b. Pete is drinking something cold because he is hot.
   ____ c. Pete is asking someone to join him in a drink.

5. decide   decided

   If you cannot _____ on what to wear, I will do it for you.
   The word you wrote means
   ____ a. make up your mind.
   ____ b. think about.
   ____ c. choose.

Check your answers with the key on page 139.

35

SEQUENCE C-9

D   COMPLETING THE SENTENCES

Choose a word from the box that best completes each sentence. Write it on the line.

decide	face	imagine	invite	practice
or	*or*	*or*	*or*	*or*
decided	faced	imagined	invited	practiced

1. Can you _____ being almost seven feet tall!

2. Did you _____ Beth to your house?

3. I _____ the wall while my friends hid.

4. Anthony _____ his talk until he knew every word.

5. I have _____ to go to the country for two weeks this summer.

Check your answers with the key on page 139.

E   USING THE SKILL

Underline the word that best completes each sentence.

1. Clara is very **excited excitement** about her new job.

2. If you keep **joked joking** around, you'll never get to sleep.

3. Stan was very **please pleased** with the present I gave him.

4. We **time timed** the horses when they raced.

5. Walter **whistle whistled** a happy song.

Check your answers with the key on page 139.

F   SUPPLEMENTARY WRITING EXERCISE

The ten new words that were taught in this lesson are:

autumn	danger	decided	excitement	gun
imagined	invited	less	practiced	shot

Choose any three of your new words from the box and write them in sentences.

1. _____

2. _____

3. _____

Look at the words in the column at the right. Choose the correct word and write it in the blank to best complete the sentence.

Check and Write

1. Tommy was _____ very early this morning. awake   faithful   curious

2. The mouse _____ in a hole in the corner. gathered   trusted   disappeared

3. Mrs. Star _____ why she would be late. signaled   explained   warned

4. Don't _____ to write to me from your new home. forget   trade   spin

5. The lost boy _____ where he lived. pretended   sank   forgot

6. Bill _____ how to cook from his father. repeated   tested   learned

7. Did you _____ your money? lose   welcome   unite

8. I _____ to return your book as soon as I finish it. scream   promise   notice

9. Roger _____ for help. feared   hammered   screamed

10. Marcia will be _____ next week. twenty   foolish   gentle

11. I'm sorry, but I _____ your name. spoke   forgot   ordered

12. "Are you _____?" whispered Sally from her bed. ripe   tender   awake

13. There are _____ children in my class. half   twenty   free

14. You must always keep a _____ that you make. promise   mistake   scream

15. Mr. Harris _____ how bees gather food. respected   frowned   explained

16. My keys were on this table and now they have _____. formed   disappeared   gathered

17. Carol _____ how to swim last summer. learned   appeared   borrowed

18. The fire trucks _____ through the city. cheered   screamed   drifted

19. How could you _____ where you put your coat? arrange   discover   forget

20. Henry thinks our team will _____ today's game. lose   boil   crack

awake (ə wāk′), 1. wake oneself up; arouse oneself. 2. not asleep. *v.,* **awoke** or **awaked, awak ing,** *adj.*

dis ap pear (dis ə pir′), pass from sight or from existence; be lost: *The little dog disappeared down the road. When spring comes the snow disappears. v.*

ex plain (eks plān′), 1. make plain; tell the meaning of; tell how to do: *The teacher explained long division to the class.* 2. state the cause of; give reasons for: *Can somebody explain Maud's absence? v.*

for get (fər get′), 1. let go out of the mind; fail to remember. 2. fail to think of; fail to do, take notice, etc. *v.,* **for got, for got ten** or **for got, for get ting.**

learn (lėrn), 1. gain knowledge or skill: *Some children learn slowly.* 2. find out; come to know: *He learned that ¼ + ¼ = ½.* 3. find out about; gain knowledge of: *She is learning history and geography.* 4. become able by study or practice: *In school we learn to read. v.,* **learned** or **learnt, learn ing.**

prom ise (prom′is), 1. words said, binding a person to do or not to do something: *A man of honor always keeps his promise.* 2. give one's word; give a promise: *He promised to stay till we came.* 3. that which gives hope of success: *a pupil of promise in music.* 5. give hope; give hope of: *The rainbow promises fair weather. n., v.,* **prom ised, prom is ing.**

scream (skrēm), 1. make a loud, sharp, piercing cry. People scream in fright, in anger, and in sudden pain. 2. a loud, sharp, piercing cry. *v., n.*

B USING CONTEXT CLUES

Place an X *in front of each correct answer. The word may be used correctly in one or both of the sentences.*

1. If Joyce shows much promise as a dancer,
   ____ a. Joyce is not dancing too well.
   ____ b. Joyce should be a very good dancer.

2. Which of the following sentences uses the underlined word correctly?
   ____ a. Joshua awakes every morning at six.
   ____ b. It seemed as if I were awake all night.

3. Which of the following sentences uses the underlined word correctly?
   ____ a. "How did you get here?" explained Vera.
   ____ b. Can you explain why you are late?

4. Which of the following sentences uses the underlined word correctly?
   ____ a. I learned Phyllis how to make those cookies.
   ____ b. Paul learned how to swim in one day.

5. People scream when they are
   ____ a. afraid.
   ____ b. hurt.

Check your answers with the key on page 140.

C CHECKING THE MEANING

Read the words in the boxes. Choose the word that best completes the sentence under them. Write that word on the line. Then complete the next sentence by placing an X in front of the correct answer.

1. | disappear | | disappeared |

   The little boy _____ from his mother's side.
   From this sentence, you know that
   ____ a. the mother could no longer see her little boy.
   ____ b. the little boy had gone for a walk.
   ____ c. the little boy could no longer see his mother.

2. | forget | | forgot |

   Mark _____ to buy a present for June.
   The word you wrote means
   ____ a. didn't want.
   ____ b. didn't learn.
   ____ c. didn't remember.

3. | scream | | screamed |

   Thomas _____ at the man who hit his car.
   From this sentence, you know that
   ____ a. Thomas was afraid.
   ____ b. Thomas was hurt.
   ____ c. Thomas was angry.

4. | promise | | promised |

   Did you _____ to dance with Carl?
   The word you wrote means
   ____ a. give your word.
   ____ b. give hope.
   ____ c. do it well.

5. | learn | | learned |

   When did you _____ that Angelo bought a new house?
   The word you wrote means
   ____ a. teach.
   ____ b. find out.
   ____ c. practice.

Check your answers with the key on page 140.

SEQUENCE C-10

D   COMPLETING THE SENTENCES

Choose a word from the box that best completes each sentence. Write it on the line.

disappear	explain	learn	open	scream
or	*or*	*or*	*or*	*or*
disappeared	explained	learned	opened	screamed

1. Mario wants to _____ to be a good basketball player.

2. Nanette _____ the door and let the dog in.

3. I watched the girl run until she _____ behind a house.

4. Please _____ to me how the telephone works.

5. Chang _____ at his dog as it ran into the street.

Check your answers with the key on page 140.

E   USING THE SKILL

Underline the word that best completes each sentence.

1. Emily **answer answered** the telephone quickly.

2. Rudy **wonder wondered** what it would be like to be a fireman.

3. Why must you **shout shouted** every time you talk to me?

4. Mr. Philips **point pointed** out the thief to the policeman.

5. Have you ever **hunt hunted** for deer?

Check your answers with the key on page 140.

F   SUPPLEMENTARY WRITING EXERCISE

The ten new words that were taught in this lesson are:

awake	disappeared	explained	forget	forgot
learned	loss	promise	screamed	twenty

Choose any three of your new words from the box and write them in sentences.

1. _____

2. _____

3. _____

A	LEARNING THE WORDS

Look at the words in the column at the right. Choose the correct word and write it in the blank to best complete the sentence.

Check and Write

1. The _____ was in the big parade yesterday.

army	banana	example

2. I am reading about the _____ of America.

bargain	discovery	treasure

3. The horse _____ the heavy wagon behind him.

whipped	planned	dragged

4. To be invited to the White House is an _____.

honor	offer	hour

5. What _____ is that man speaking?

model	form	language

6. The racer hoped to win a gold _____.

medal	nickel	pea

7. Yesterday, two girls _____ all the way to school.

tipped	skipped	snapped

8. The horse _____ toward the fence.

spinned	spotted	trotted

9. Lila _____ the baby in a heavy blanket.

wrapped	fanned	stirred

10. Have you _____ a letter to Kate?

spoken	written	replied

11. We hope to _____ Joe at a dinner tonight.

poke	honor	manage

12. Jimmy has to carry a gun in the _____.

army	bedroom	church

13. I have just _____ a short story.

understood	touched	written

14. Most people in America speak only one _____.

language	nation	holiday

15. Irv _____ the television set across the floor.

pinned	hugged	dragged

16. The horses _____ around the circus ring.

napped	trotted	clipped

17. Do you like the way I _____ this package?

wrapped	grabbed	dipped

18. Lola wears a shiny _____ around her neck.

potato	rattle	medal

19. The _____ of the diamond mine made us rich.

truth	price	discovery

20. Last spring, squirrels _____ across the tree tops.

nodded	skipped	dripped

ar my (är′mē), 1. an organized group of soldiers trained and armed for war. 2. any organized group of people: *the Salvation Army.* 3. multitude; very large number: *an army of ants. n., pl.* **ar mies.**

drag (drag), 1. pull or move along heavily or slowly; pull or draw along the ground: *A team of horses dragged the big log out of the forest.* 2. go too slowly: *A piece of music played too slowly drags. Time drags when you have nothing to do.* 3. pull a net, hook, harrow, etc., over or along for some purpose: *People drag a lake for fish or for a drowned person's body. v.,* **dragged, drag ging,** *n.*

skip (skip), 1. leap lightly; spring; jump: *Lambs skip in the fields.* 2. leap lightly over: *Girls skip rope.* 3. pass over; omit: *Lola skips the hard words when she reads.* 4. advance in school, by passing one or more grades: *Jean skipped a grade last year.* 5. change quickly from one task, pleasure, subject, etc., to another. *v.,* **skipped, skip ping,** *n.*

trot (trot), 1. go by lifting the right forefoot and the left hind foot at about the same time: *Horses trot.* 2. ride at a trot. 3. run, but not fast: *The child trotted along after his mother. v.,* **trot ted, trot ting,** *n.*

wrap (rap), 1. wind or fold as a covering: *Wrap a blanket around the baby.* 2. cover by winding or folding something around: *The mountain peak is wrapped in clouds.* 3. **Wrapped up in** sometimes means devoted to; thinking chiefly of: *Mrs. Jones is wrapped up in her children.* 4. cover and tie up. *v.,* **wrapped** or **wrapt, wrap ping,** *n.*

write (rīt), 1. make letters or words with pen, pencil, or chalk: *You can read and write.* 2. put down the words of: *Write your name.* 3. make up stories, books, etc.; compose: *Mr. Blank writes for the magazines.* 4. show plainly: *Fear was written on his face.* 5. Some special meanings are: **write down,** put into writing. **write out,** put into writing. **write up, 1.** write a description or account of. **2.** write in detail. *v.,* **wrote, writ ten, writ ing.**

B   USING CONTEXT CLUES

Place an X *in front of each correct answer. The word may be used correctly in one or both of the sentences.*

1. If some men were <u>dragging</u> a lake for a car,
    ____ a.   they were slowly pulling the car into the lake.
    ____ b.   they were pulling something through the water to find the car.

2. If Carol <u>wrote up</u> her trip for the school paper,
    ____ a.   she wrote a make-believe story.
    ____ b.   she wrote about her trip from beginning to end.

3. Which of the following sentences uses the underlined word correctly?
    ____ a.   Lorraine <u>skipped</u> up the steps to her house.
    ____ b.   Herbie <u>skipped</u> that story in the book.

4. If Janet was <u>wrapped up</u> in making a blanket,
    ____ a.   she was covered with the blanket.
    ____ b.   she was doing nothing else.

5. Which of the following sentences uses the underlined word correctly?
    ____ a.   <u>Write out</u> what you want and I will buy it for you.
    ____ b.   John has <u>written</u> many beautiful songs.

Check your answers with the key on page 140.

C CHECKING THE MEANING

Read the words in the boxes. Choose the word that best completes the sentence under them. Write that word on the line. Then complete the next sentence by placing an X in front of the correct answer.

1. | armies | | army |

There was an _____ of people waiting to see the new play.
The word you wrote means
____ a. a large number of people.
____ b. a small number of people.
____ c. people trained and armed for war.

2. | trot | | trotting |

Horses were _____ across the field.
The word you wrote means
____ a. jumping high.
____ b. running quickly.
____ c. running slowly.

3. | skip | | skipped |

Anthony _____ his corn and ate his hot dog.
The word you wrote means that
____ a. Anthony liked the corn.
____ b. Anthony jumped with his corn.
____ c. Anthony didn't eat his corn.

4. | wrap | | wrapped |

I want to _____ this package and mail it.
The word you wrote means
____ a. think only of.
____ b. cover and tie up.
____ c. fold.

5. | drag | | dragged |

Yesterday just _____ on by.
From this sentence, you know that
____ a. it was a good day.
____ b. the day passed quickly.
____ c. the day passed slowly.

Check your answers with the key on page 140.

SEQUENCE C-11

D COMPLETING THE SENTENCES

Choose a word from the box that best completes each sentence. Write it on the line.

drag	skip	slip	trot	wrap
or	*or*	*or*	*or*	*or*
dragged	skipped	slipped	trotted	wrapped

1. Please _____ that page and go on to the next one.

2. Ellen _____ on the banana skin and broke her arm.

3. Did you _____ Kim's present?

4. We take the horses for a _____ every day.

5. The boy _____ the sled up the hill.

Check your answers with the key on page 140.

E USING THE SKILL

Underline the word that best completes each sentence.

1. What do you **plan planned** to do when you get out of school?

2. The dog sat up and **beg begged** for some food.

3. You must **stir stirred** the paint very well before you use it.

4. Mr. Olson **nod nodded** his head in answer to my question.

5. Harvey **drum drummed** his fingers on the table in time to the music.

Check your answers with the key on page 140.

F SUPPLEMENTARY WRITING EXERCISE

The ten new words that were taught in this lesson are:

army	discovery	dragged	honor	language
medal	skipped	trotted	wrapped	written

Choose any three of your new words from the box and write them in sentences.

1. _____

2. _____

3. _____

Look at the words in the column at the right. Choose the correct
word and write it in the blank to best complete the sentence.

Check and Write

1. It was time to get _____ the train.

| among | aboard | against |

2. I am proud to be an _____.

| American | insect | eagle |

3. The moon does not _____ every night.

| appear | spread | circle |

4. Judy can _____ boats from soap.

| chop | hook | carve |

5. When we saw our team win, we all _____.

| wandered | cheered | gathered |

6. To make paper, many trees have to be _____ down.

| chopped | tipped | grabbed |

7. My father _____ all the money that I spend.

| sweeps | forms | earns |

8. In the last year, I have _____ taller.

| drifted | grown | remained |

9. My sister always tries to _____ her money.

| save | mix | freeze |

10. My new ring _____ when the light hit it.

| trembled | sparkled | aged |

11. Walter likes to _____ faces in wood.

| bend | divide | carve |

12. My plant has _____ flowers in the past week.

| grown | crept | led |

13. I _____ these branches for firewood.

| slapped | chopped | tapped |

14. We got _____ the train just before it left.

| upon | against | aboard |

15. The car _____ after I cleaned it.

| chuckled | nibbled | sparkled |

16. Mike _____ almost ten dollars an hour.

| earns | unites | orders |

17. I like to _____ letters from my friends.

| mark | save | lift |

18. The _____ Indian has been here a long time.

| Thursday | Monday | American |

19. In the spring, flowers _____ almost like magic.

| appear | attack | arrange |

20. We all went to the baseball game and _____.

| cracked | cheered | traveled |

SEQUENCE C-12

Amer i can (ə mer'ə kən), 1. of the United States; belonging to the United States: *an American citizen.* 2. citizen of the United States. 3. person born or living in America. *adj., n.*

ap pear (ə pir'), 1. be seen: *One by one the stars appear.* 2. seem; look: *The apple appeared sound, but it was rotten.* 3. be published: *This poet's last book appeared a year ago.* 4. show or present oneself publicly or formally: *A person accused of crime must appear before the court. v.*

cheer (chir), 1. to comfort; make glad: *It cheered the old woman to have us visit her.* 2. "Cheer up!" means "Don't be sad; be glad!" 3. a shout of sympathy and support or praise: *Give three cheers for the boys who won the game for us.* 4. urge on by cheers or other means: *Everyone cheered our team. n., v.*

chop (chop), 1. cut by blows: *to chop wood with an ax.* 2. cut into small pieces: *to chop up cabbage.* 3. cutting blow. 4. move in small, jerky waves. *v.,* **chopped, chop ping,** *n.*

earn (ėrn), 1. get in return for work or service; be paid: *Mary gives her mother half of what she earns.* 2. do enough work for; do good enough work for: *Donald is paid more than he really earns. v.*

save (sāv), 1. make safe; keep or rescue from harm, danger, hurt, loss, etc.: *The dog saved the boy's life. The woman saved her jewels from the fire.* 2. lay aside: *to save money. She saves pieces of string.* 3. keep from spending or wasting: *Save your strength.* 4. prevent; make less: *to save work, to save trouble.* 5. treat carefully to lessen wear, weariness, etc.: *Large print saves one's eyes. v.,* **saved, sav ing.**

B USING CONTEXT CLUES

Place an X in front of each correct answer. The word may be used correctly in one or both of the sentences.

1. If Jonathon's story appeared in the school paper,
   ____ a. the story was printed in the paper.
   ____ b. the story was liked.

2. Which of the following sentences uses the underlined word correctly?
   ____ a. Ray found that chopping wood is hard work.
   ____ b. Chop the fruit before you put it in the bowl.

3. Which of the following sentences uses the underlined word correctly?
   ____ a. The thief broke into our save.
   ____ b. Louis saved Judy the trouble of walking the dog.

4. If George cheered the home team,
   ____ a. he made them feel at home.
   ____ b. he shouted to show he wanted them to win.

5. If my set of dishes is American,
   ____ a. it is in America.
   ____ b. it was made in America.

Check your answers with the key on page 140.

C CHECKING THE MEANING

Read the words in the boxes. Choose the word that best completes the sentence under them. Write that word on the line. Then complete the next sentence by placing an X in front of the correct answer.

1. | America | | American |

Hans became an _____ after being here three years.
From this sentence, you know that
____ a. Hans was born in America.
____ b. Hans decided to live always in America.
____ c. Hans no longer lives in America.

2. | earn | | earned |

Fay does not _____ enough money to live on.
From this sentence, you know that
____ a. Fay is paid too little for the work she does.
____ b. Fay works hard for the money she makes.
____ c. Fay doesn't make enough money to buy the things she needs.

3. | cheer | | cheered |

Mike hoped to _____ Annette after the bad news came.
The word you wrote means
____ a. make glad.
____ b. fill with fear.
____ c. shout loudly.

4. | appear | | appeared |

The woman _____ to be well.
The word you wrote means
____ a. seemed.
____ b. be seen.
____ c. showed.

5. | save | | saved |

Were you able to _____ anything from the fire?
The word you wrote means
____ a. put aside.
____ b. keep from harm.
____ c. not spend.

Check your answers with the key on page 140.

D COMPLETING THE SENTENCES

Choose a word from the box that best completes each sentence. Write it on the line.

carve	cheer	chop	earn	sparkle
or	*or*	*or*	*or*	*or*
carves	cheered	chopped	earns	sparkled

1. What are you going to _____ out of your soap?

2. The stars _____ in the sky last night.

3. How much money do you _____ every week?

4. Tad _____ for his team every time they played.

5. Dick _____ wood for the fire.

Check your answers with the key on page 140.

E USING THE SKILL

Underline the word that best completes each sentence.

1. Paula always **repeat repeats** what she says.

2. There have been many **crash crashes** at this corner.

3. How do you **manage managed** to keep such a nice house?

4. The airplane kept **circled circling** until it could land.

5. Alex **pin pinned** the flowers on Sally's dress.

Check your answers with the key on page 140.

F SUPPLEMENTARY WRITING EXERCISE

The ten new words that were taught in this lesson are:

aboard	American	appear	carve	cheered
chopped	earns	grown	save	sparkled

Choose any three of your new words from the box and write them in sentences.

1. _____

2. _____

3. _____

Look at the words in the column at the right. Choose the correct word and write it in the blank to best complete the sentence.

Check and Write

1. The children went to sleep in their parents' _____.

tunnel   sleigh   bedroom

2. After dinner, I _____ the dishes.

dried   copied   satisfied

3. The lake will _____ in the moonlight.

gather   model   glitter

4. The dog tried to _____ my friend by his shirt.

hound   grab   wreck

5. Kim is very _____ in the morning.

lively   narrow   greedy

6. My brother _____ a girl he knew as a child.

copied   married   dried

7. I am very _____ when I do something well.

busied   married   satisfied

8. Mary always _____ hard in school.

studied   replied   dirtied

9. There was a _____ storm last night.

famous   delicious   sudden

10. I hope _____ having a good time.

you've   you're   I'd

11. The _____ of my gold caught my eye.

glitter   patch   pound

12. When I go riding, I like a _____ horse.

stiff   smooth   lively

13. My teacher is _____ with my schoolwork.

carried   satisfied   copied

14. "This is going to be my _____," said Marian.

bedroom   arrow   carrot

15. If I _____ the song, I could sing it better.

dirtied   dried   studied

16. All of a _____ , the sun came out from behind a cloud.

swallow   sudden   startle

17. You should not talk while _____ eating.

you're   we'll   I'll

18. Teddy's parents have been _____ for ten years.

replied   married   busied

19. When you play basketball, _____ the ball and throw it.

grease   lose   grab

20. I like _____ fruits the best.

dried   dirtied   satisfied

dry (drī), **1.** not wet; not moist: *Dust is dry.* **2.** make dry by wiping, draining, or heating, **3.** not giving milk: *The cow is dry.* **4.** having no water. **5.** having little or no rain: *a dry climate.* **6.** thirsty; wanting a drink. *adj.,* **dri er, dri est,** *v.,* **dried, dry ing.**

glit ter (glit'ər), **1.** sparkle; seem to have shining bits in it. **2.** shine with a bright, sparkling light: *The jewels and new coins glittered.* **3.** bright, sparkling light. **4.** be bright and showy. *v., n.*

live ly (līv'lē), **1.** full of life and spirit; active. **2.** exciting. **3.** bouncing well and quickly: *a lively ball. adj.,* **live li er, live li est,** *adv.*

grab (grab), **1.** snatch; seize suddenly: *The dog grabbed the meat and ran.* **2.** a snatching; a sudden seizing. *v.,* **grabbed, grab bing,** *n.*

mar ry (mar'ē), **1.** join as husband and wife: *The minister married them.* **2.** take as husband or wife: *James married Ida.* **3.** give in marriage: *She has married all her daughters.* **4.** bring together in any close union. *v.,* **mar ried, mar ry ing.**

sat is fy (sat'is fī), **1.** give enough to fulfill (desires, hopes, demands, etc.); put an end to (needs, wants, etc.): *He satisfied his hunger with bread and milk.* **2.** make contented; please: *Are you satisfied now?* **3.** pay; make right: *After the accident he satisfied all claims for the damage he had caused.* **4.** convince: *The teacher is satisfied that his statement is true. v.,* **sat is fied, sat is fy ing.**

study (stud'ē), **1.** make an effort to learn: *Helen studied her spelling lesson for half an hour. Joseph is studying to be a doctor.* **2.** room to study in: *The minister was reading in his study.* **3.** give care and thought to; try hard: *The grocer studies to please his customers.* **4.** examine carefully: *We studied the map to find the shortest road home. n., pl.* **stud ies,** *v.,* **stud ied, stud y ing.**

B   USING CONTEXT CLUES

Place an X in front of each correct answer. The word may be used correctly in one or both of the sentences.

1. If Mr. and Mrs. Judson have <u>married</u> all their children,
    ____ a.   they have seen all their children find husbands or wives.
    ____ b.   they live with their children and their husbands and wives.

2. If Diane was so <u>dry</u> that she drank four glasses of water,
    ____ a.   Diane was not wet.
    ____ b.   Diane was thirsty.

3. If Dominic is in a <u>study</u>,
    ____ a.   he is in a room.
    ____ b.   he is trying to learn something.

4. If Otto is <u>satisfied</u> that Rosa is not lying,
    ____ a.   he is sure that what she says is true.
    ____ b.   he is pleased that what she says is true.

5. Which of the following sentences uses the underlined word correctly?
    ____ a.   That was a very <u>lively</u> race.
    ____ b.   The man was sleeping <u>lively</u>.

Check your answers with the key on page 141.

| C   CHECKING THE MEANING |

Read the words in the boxes. Choose the word that best completes the sentence under them. Write that word on the line. Then complete the next sentence by placing an X in front of the correct answer.

1. | dried | | dry |

It is very _____ where I live.
The word you wrote means
____ a. having hot summers.
____ b. having cold winters.
____ c. having little rain.

2. | grab | | grabbed |

The man _____ the woman's arm.
The word you wrote means
____ a. held tightly.
____ b. took hold quickly.
____ c. hurt.

3. | studied | | study |

The builder _____ the drawing of the house for a long time.
From this sentence, you know that
____ a. the builder looked at the drawing carefully.
____ b. the builder was going to build a new house.
____ c. the builder liked to look at pictures.

4. | satisfied | | satisfy |

Did you _____ your doctor's bill?
The word you wrote means
____ a. pay.
____ b. please.
____ c. take.

5. | studies | | studying |

Arthur _____ ways of satisfying the people he works for.
The word you wrote means
____ a. tries to teach.
____ b. looks at quickly.
____ c. thinks hard and carefully.

Check your answers with the key on page 141.

SEQUENCE C-13

D   COMPLETING THE SENTENCES

Choose a word from the box that best completes each sentence. Write it on the line.

cry	dry	marry	satisfy	study
or	or	or	or	or
cried	dried	married	satisfied	studied

1. Lenny _____ his mother by eating the food she had made.

2. Susan and Josh plan to be _____ in July.

3. How long are you going to let the baby _____?

4. Charles helped Theresa _____ the dishes.

5. John _____ the map as he planned his trip.

Check your answers with the key on page 141.

E   USING THE SKILL

Underline the word that best completes each sentence.

1. Can you **carried carry** all these packages?

2. I am waiting for a **replied reply** to my letter.

3. Frank **emptied empty** the bottle of milk.

4. The boxers **readied ready** for their fight.

5. If you didn't **hurried hurry** so much, you wouldn't be so tired.

Check your answers with the key on page 141.

F   SUPPLEMENTARY WRITING EXERCISE

The ten new words that were taught in this lesson are:

bedroom	dried	glitter	grab	lively
married	satisfied	studied	sudden	you're

Choose any three of your new words from the box and write them in sentences.

1. _____

2. _____

3. _____

A   LEARNING THE WORDS

Look at the words in the column at the right. Choose the correct word and write it in the blank to best complete the sentence.

Check and Write

1. An _____ storm knocked down these trees.

    eager   awful   extra

2. I have just _____ to pack for my trip.

    begun   continued   deserved

3. The bright light was _____ me.

    trusting   spoiling   blinding

4. I _____ every night before I go to bed.

    exercise   melt   gaze

5. Mary is _____ to start school next year.

    growling   expecting   floating

6. There was a _____ of men sitting in the park.

    patch   tribe   group

7. Nick thought that _____ nails was hard work.

    hammering   repairing   pressing

8. The squirrel hid in the _____ of a tree.

    sail   hollow   hoop

9. I have never _____ anyone like Hank.

    shot   sold   known

10. Betsy was _____ her friends with water.

    spraying   lowering   allowing

11. I get most of my _____ by running.

    fear   danger   exercise

12. They are _____ rain today.

    explaining   expecting   earning

13. Tony is _____ a piece of wood into the ground.

    hammering   dashing   cracking

14. Something is stuck inside the large _____ pipe.

    cloth   brick   hollow

15. Martin is _____ the chairs with paint.

    boiling   spraying   forming

16. The sun was _____ me as I drove home.

    blinding   pressing   signaling

17. Matt has just _____ to learn how to read.

    understand   begun   imagined

18. The dog seemed to have _____ he was very sick.

    planned   noted   known

19. The food we ate last night was _____ !

    awful   impossible   foolish

20. That _____ of boys is always getting into trouble.

    load   bundle   group

be gin (bi gin'), **1.** do the first part; start: *We will begin work soon.* **2.** come into being: *The club began two years ago.* **3.** bring into being: *Two brothers began the club ten years ago.* **4.** be near; come near: *That suit doesn't even begin to fit you.* *v.,* **be gan, be gun, be gin ning.**

blind (blind), **1.** not able to see. **2.** take away one's sight; make blind. **3.** hard to see: *a blind track.* **4.** without judgment or good sense. **5.** without an opening: *a blind wall.* **6.** with only one opening: *a blind alley.* *adj., v., n.*

ex er cise (ek'sər sīz), **1.** practice; active use: *Exercise is good for body and mind.* **2.** make use of: *Exercise caution in crossing the street.* **3.** something that gives practice: *Do the exercises at the end of the lesson.* **4.** procedure; ceremony: *the opening exercises in a Sunday school.* **5.** perform: *The mayor exercises the duties of his office.* *v.,* **ex er cised, ex er cis ing,** *n.*

group (grüp), **1.** a number of persons or things together: *A group of children were playing tag.* **2.** number of persons or things belonging or classed together: *Wheat, rye, and oats belong to the grain group.*

3. form into a group: *The children grouped themselves at the monkey's cage.* **4.** put in a group. *n., v.*

ham mer (ham'ər), **1.** a tool with a metal head and a handle, used for driving nails, etc. **2.** drive, hit, or work with a hammer. **3.** beat into shape with a hammer: *The metal was hammered into ornaments.* **4.** force by many efforts: *Arithmetic has to be hammered into that dull boy's head.* *n., v.*

hol low (hol'ō), **1.** having nothing, or only air, inside; empty; with a hole inside; not solid: *A tube or pipe is hollow. Most rubber balls are hollow.* **2.** bowl-shaped; cup-shaped: *a hollow dish for vegetables.* **3.** a hollow place; a hole: *a hollow in the road.* **4.** dull; as if coming from something hollow: *a hollow voice, a hollow groan, the hollow boom of a foghorn.* **5.** deep and sunken: *A starving person has hollow cheeks. adj., n., v.*

know (nō), **1.** tell apart from others: *He knows many kinds of birds.* **2.** be acquainted with: *I know her very well.* **3.** have the facts and be sure that they are true: *We know that 2 and 2 are 4.* **4.** have knowledge: *Mother knows from experience how to cook.* *v.,* **knew, known, know ing.**

B   USING CONTEXT CLUES

Place an X in front of each correct answer. The word may be used correctly in one or both of the sentences.

1. If Tina <u>knows</u> almost everyone who lives in her apartment building very well,
    ____ a.   she can tell one from the other.
    ____ b.   she is sure that what they say is true.

2. If Barbara has finished all the <u>exercises</u> at the end of her book,
    ____ a.   she gets good marks.
    ____ b.   she did something to give her practice.

3. Which of the following are <u>hollow</u>?
    ____ a.   A drum
    ____ b.   A hole

4. If school <u>began</u> two weeks ago,
    ____ a.   the school is two weeks old.
    ____ b.   the first day of school was two weeks ago.

5. If Peter <u>blindly</u> followed Judy wherever she went,
    ____ a.   Peter did not think about where he was going.
    ____ b.   Peter could not see where he was going.

Check your answers with the key on page 141.

C CHECKING THE MEANING

Read the words in the boxes. Choose the word that best completes the sentence under them. Write that word on the line. Then complete the next sentence by placing an X in front of the correct answer.

1. | group | | grouped |

   Most of the children in this _____ are six years old.
   The word you wrote means
   ____ a. a number of people together.
   ____ b. put together.
   ____ c. made into a group.

2. | hammered | | hammering |

   This pot is made of _____ iron.
   From this sentence, you know that
   ____ a. the pot is a tool used to hammer nails.
   ____ b. the iron was beaten into shape with a hammer.
   ____ c. an iron was used to beat the pot into its shape.

3. | blind | | blinding |

   The _____ boy was helped from the room.
   From this sentence, you know that
   ____ a. the room had only one door.
   ____ b. the boy cannot see.
   ____ c. the boy was not very smart.

4. | beginning | | begun |

   Frank had not _____ to read the book when he had to return it.
   The word you wrote means
   ____ a. did for the very first time.
   ____ b. brought into being.
   ____ c. started.

5. | exercised | | exercising |

   I am _____ my right as your mother to tell you what to do.
   The word you wrote means
   ____ a. doing or carrying out.
   ____ b. working or playing.
   ____ c. making or building.

Check your answers with the key on page 141.

D COMPLETING THE SENTENCES

Choose a word from the box that best completes each sentence. Write it on the line.

blind	expect	hammer	spray	storm
or	*or*	*or*	*or*	*or*
blinding	expecting	hammering	spraying	storming

1. How long are you _____ to stay here?

2. The _____ light hurt my eyes.

3. Timothy wants to _____ this chair with green paint.

4. Use a _____ to nail these two pieces of wood together.

5. A sudden _____ made driving very hard.

Check your answers with the key on page 141.

E USING THE SKILL

Underline the word that best completes each sentence.

1. All in all, it was a very **disappointed disappointing** day.

2. Philip **attacked attacking** his food as if he hadn't eaten in months.

3. I still have some **iron ironing** to do.

4. Marcia is **pretended pretending** to be asleep.

5. Do you know when Murray's ship **sailing sails**?

Check your answers with the key on page 141.

F SUPPLEMENTARY WRITING EXERCISE

The ten new words that were taught in this lesson are:

awful	begun	blinding	exercise	expecting
group	hammering	hollow	known	spraying

Choose any three of your new words from the box and write them in sentences.

1. _____

2. _____

3. _____

Look at the words in the column at the right. Choose the correct word and write it in the blank to best complete the sentence.

Check and Write

1. When will you be _____ the winner?

deserving   dividing   announcing

2. Take the _____ out of the fireplace.

ashes   diamond   nickel

3. Are you _____ that you left your glasses in school?

sold   certain   taught

4. How much did that book _____?

cost   tap   stretch

5. Don't try _____ your child to eat.

choosing   arranging   forcing

6. The policeman was a _____ to the people he saved.

sailor   hero   doctor

7. Who is the _____ of this company?

president   passenger   parent

8. Who is _____ the drowning swimmer?

exercising   greasing   rescuing

9. I am drawing a country _____.

nation   scene   coast

10. Stop _____ and it will be easier to swim.

struggling   behaving   choosing

11. After the fire, all that was left was _____.

chocolate   space   ashes

12. That country will soon get a new _____.

promise   president   rooster

13. Philip is _____ to learn how to play the piano.

struggling   deserving   noticing

14. Many things _____ more today than they once did.

match   prove   cost

15. Can you picture the _____ I am talking about?

slide   scene   steam

16. They are _____ the news right now.

announcing   arranging   amusing

17. Daniel Boone was a great American _____.

beauty   body   hero

18. There is a _____ person I hope to see at the party.

common   certain   complete

19. Stop _____ Harold to do things.

handling   managing   forcing

20. Be quick and daring when you are _____ someone.

rescuing   promising   serving

cer tain (sėrt′n), 1. sure: *It is certain that 3 and 2 do not make 6.* 2. some: *Certain plants will not grow in this country.* 3. known but not named: *A certain person gave our church $1000. adj.*

cost (kôst), 1. price paid: *The cost of this hat was $10.* 2. loss; sacrifice: *The poor fox escaped from the trap at the cost of a leg. n., v., cost, cost ing.*

force (fôrs), 1. power; strength. 2. make (a person) act against his will; make do by force: *Give it to me at once, or I will force you to.* 3. get or take by force: *Tom forced his way in.* 4. break through: *to force a door. n., v., forced, forc ing.*

res cue (res′kū), 1. save from danger or harm; free; deliver: *The dog rescued the child from drowning.* 2. saving or freeing from harm or danger: *The fireman was praised for his brave rescue of the children*

in the burning house. *A dog was chasing our cat when Mary came to the resuce. v., res cued, res cu ing, n.*

scene (sēn), 1. the time, place, circumstances, etc., of a play or story: *The scene is laid in Boston in the year 1775.* 2. the painted screens, hangings, etc., used in a theater to represent places: *The scene represents a city street.* 3. part of an act of a play: *The king comes to the castle in Act 1, Scene 2.* 4. a particular incident of a play: *The trial scene is the most exciting one in "The Merchant of Venice."* 5. view; picture: *The white sailboats in the blue water made a pretty scene.* 6. show of strong feeling: *The child kicked and screamed and made such a scene on the train that his mother was ashamed of him. n.*

strug gle (strug′l), 1. make great efforts with the body; try hard; work hard against difficulties: *The swimmer struggled against the tide. Many men have to struggle for a living.* 2. great effort; hard work. 3. fighting. *v., strug gled, strug gling, n.*

B USING CONTEXT CLUES

Place an X *in front of each correct answer. The word may be used correctly in one or both of the sentences.*

1. Which of the following sentences uses the underlined word correctly?
   - ____ a. A policeman <u>rescued</u> Mrs. Dominic when she fell into the lake.
   - ____ b. The swimmer <u>rescuing</u> in the water.

2. If Florence was <u>certain</u> that what she ate made her sick,
   - ____ a. she was sure of what it was.
   - ____ b. she ate only some of it.

3. If a policeman stopped a <u>struggle</u> soon after it started,
   - ____ a. the policeman tried hard to stop a fight.
   - ____ b. the policeman stopped a fight.

4. Which of the following sentences uses the underlined word correctly?
   - ____ a. Bill's <u>cost</u> came off his leg a week ago.
   - ____ b. What is the <u>cost</u> of this dress?

5. When the thief <u>forced</u> open the door,
   - ____ a. he broke through the door.
   - ____ b. he showed he was very angry.

Check your answers with the key on page 141.

C CHECKING THE MEANING

Read the words in the boxes. Choose the word that best completes the sentence under them.
Write that word on the line. Then complete the next sentence by placing an X in front of the
correct answer.

1. | scene | | scenes |

   Little Alice made an awful _____ when her mother wouldn't buy
   ice cream.
   The word you wrote means
   ____ a. a part of a play.
   ____ b. a show of strong feeling.
   ____ c. a picture.

2. | certain | | certainly |

   There is a _____ man here who was not invited.
   The word you wrote means
   ____ a. sure.
   ____ b. some.
   ____ c. known, but not named.

3. | forced | | forcing |

   The water _____ its way in through the hole in the boat.
   From this sentence, you know that
   ____ a. the water broke through the hole.
   ____ b. the water was very strong.
   ____ c. the water made the hole in the boat.

4. | cost | | costs |

   The boy's carelessness _____ him his arm.
   From this sentence, you know that
   ____ a. a lot of money was needed to save the boy's arm.
   ____ b. the boy lost his arm.
   ____ c. the boy paid a lot of money for a new arm.

5. | struggle | | struggled |

   Martin had to _____ to win the race.
   The word you wrote means
   ____ a. work hard.
   ____ b. run fast.
   ____ c. practice often.

Check your answers with the key on page 141.

SEQUENCE C-15

D   COMPLETING THE SENTENCES

Choose a word from the box that best completes each sentence. Write it on the line.

announce	force	rescue	scare	struggle
or	*or*	*or*	*or*	*or*
announcing	forcing	rescuing	scaring	struggling

1. Charlie will _____ his plans tonight.

2. Arnie is _____ to finish his work before five o'clock.

3. That was an awful _____ you gave me!

4. The wind's _____ pulled out many trees by their roots.

5. Do you think the hero will _____ his friends?

Check your answers with the key on page 141.

E   USING THE SKILL

Underline the word that best completes each sentence.

1. Brian is **shake shaking** from the cold.

2. The thief **escaped escaping** from the house before the policeman could get in.

3. My car has a terrible **rattle rattling**.

4. That chimney sends out too much **smoke smoking**.

5. The **dare daring** rescue of the boy was seen by many people.

Check your answers with the key on page 141.

F   SUPPLEMENTARY WRITING EXERCISE

The ten new words that were taught in this lesson are:

announcing	ashes	certain	cost	forcing
hero	president	rescuing	scene	struggling

Choose any three of your new words from the box and write them in sentences.

1. _____

2. _____

3. _____

A LEARNING THE WORDS

Look at the words in the column at the right. Choose the correct word and write it in the blank to best complete the sentence.

Check and Write

1. I will _____ for someone to meet you.
   address   appear   arrange

2. Rain is a welcome _____ to those living in the desert.
   bother   difference   blessing

3. Everyone started _____ when the president arrived.
   clapping   chopping   clipping

4. What is the _____ on that letter?
   extra   date   dash

5. Your ice cream is _____ on the floor.
   dragging   dripping   dipping

6. I had _____ to take my lunch to school.
   forgotten   replied   imagined

7. After winning the game, the team was _____ one another.
   nodding   hugging   drumming

8. I like to read the _____ each morning.
   newspaper   weather   piano

9. My head was _____ after my fall.
   grabbing   shedding   spinning

10. My father had a lot of _____.
    steam   wisdom   scent

11. The water is _____ onto the floor.
    snapping   splitting   dripping

12. The loud _____ hurt my ears.
    clapping   napping   planning

13. What was the _____ of the discovery of America?
    dawn   date   direction

14. Today's _____ has many good stories.
    copy   sheet   newspaper

15. John showed great _____ when he stopped the fight.
    practice   wisdom   harm

16. Have you _____ to do your homework?
    glanced   marched   forgotten

17. I always ask a _____ before I eat.
    blessing   promise   truth

18. The baby is _____ his mother.
    skipping   slipping   hugging

19. Can you _____ to leave early?
    intend   arrange   search

20. The toy top keeps _____.
    spinning   shipping   slapping

ar range (ə rānj'), 1. put in proper order: *The army is arranged for battle.* 2. settle: *Mother arranged the dispute between the two girls.* 3. plan; form plans: *Can you arrange to be at my house by six o'clock?* 4. adapt; fit: *This music for the violin is also arranged for the piano.* v., ar ranged, ar rang ing.

bless ing (bles'ing), 1. a prayer asking God to show His favor: *The priest gave them his blessing.* 2. a wish for happiness or success. 3. anything that makes people happy and contented. *n.*

clap (klap), 1. a sudden noise, such as a single burst of thunder, the sound of the hands struck together, or the sound of a loud slap. 2. make such a noise, especially with the hands: *When the show was over, we all clapped.* 3. strike with a quick blow: *He clapped his friend on the back.* *n., v.,* clapped, clap ping.

date (dāt), 1. time; a statement of a time: *1492 is the date of the discovery of America by Columbus.* 2. mark the time of; put a date on: *Please date your letter.* 3. period of time: *At that date there were no airplanes.* Out of date means out of fashion. Up to date means (1) in fashion. (2) up to the present time. 4. belong to a certain period of time; have its origin: *The oldest house in town dates from the 18th century.* 5. appointment for a certain time. *Used in common talk.* *n., v.,* dat ed, dat ing.

hug (hug), 1. put the arms around and hold close: *The girl hugs her big doll.* 2. a tight clasp with the arms: *Give mother a hug.* 3. cling firmly or fondly to: *to hug an opinion.* 4. keep close to: *The boat hugged the shore.* *v.,* hugged, hug ging, *n.*

spin (spin), 1. draw out and twist (cotton, flax, wool, etc.) into thread. 2. produce: *Sailors spin yarns about the sea.* 3. make turn around rapidly: *The boy spins his top.* 4. turn around rapidly: *The wheel spun.* 5. feel as if one were whirling around: *My head is spinning.* 6. rapid run, ride, drive, etc.: *Get your bicycle and come for a spin with me.* *v.,* spun, spin ning, *n.*

B USING CONTEXT CLUES

Place an X in front of each correct answer. The word may be used correctly in one or both of the sentences.

1. Which of the following sentences uses the underlined word correctly?
   _____ a. Pete is <u>spinning</u> a story about the war.
   _____ b. The wheel of the bicycle <u>spun</u> around and around.

2. If Nancy and Arlene <u>arranged</u> to meet for lunch,
   _____ a. they planned not to meet each other.
   _____ b. they planned to meet somewhere for lunch.

3. If Paul had a <u>date</u> last night,
   _____ a. he did something at a certain time.
   _____ b. he went to the movies.

4. Which of the following sentences uses the underlined word correctly?
   _____ a. The car <u>hugged</u> the side of the road.
   _____ b. The little girl <u>hugged</u> the doll.

5. If Mario <u>clapped</u> his hand over his mouth,
   _____ a. he was going to laugh.
   _____ b. he quickly covered his mouth.

Check your answers with the key on page 142.

C   CHECKING THE MEANING

Read the words in the boxes. Choose the word that best completes the sentence under them.
Write that word on the line. Then complete the next sentence by placing an X in front of the
correct answer.

1. | blessed | | blessing |

   Farmers think that this weather is a _____.
   From this sentence, you know that
   ____ a.   farmers are happy about the weather.
   ____ b.   farmers are not happy about the weather.
   ____ c.   farmers want more rain.

2. | arrange | | arranged |

   Harold _____ for us to sit together.
   The word you wrote means
   ____ a.   wanted.
   ____ b.   tried.
   ____ c.   planned.

3. | date | | dated |

   When was that letter _____?
   The word you wrote means
   ____ a.   a point in time.
   ____ b.   marked with the date.
   ____ c.   belonging to a certain time.

4. | spin | | spinning |

   The woman was _____ the wool.
   From this sentence, you know that
   ____ a.   the woman was telling a story.
   ____ b.   the woman was making thread.
   ____ c.   the woman was going around and around.

5. | hugged | | hugging |

   Albert is _____ his father.
   The word you wrote means
   ____ a.   staying near.
   ____ b.   pushing away.
   ____ c.   holding close.

Check your answers with the key on page 142.

D COMPLETING THE SENTENCES

Choose a word from the box that best completes each sentence. Write it on the line.

clap	drip	hug	skip	spin
or	*or*	*or*	*or*	*or*
clapping	dripping	hugging	skipping	spinning

1. The children were hopping and _____ down the street.

2. Stamp your feet and _____ your hands.

3. Give your mother a _____ and a kiss.

4. Hang up your wet clothes and let them _____ dry.

5. The boy is _____ like a top.

Check your answers with the key on page 142.

E USING THE SKILL

Underline the word that best completes each sentence.

1. I have never **slapped slapping** my dog.

2. Be careful or you will **tip tipping** over the canoe.

3. He **wrapped wrapping** a blanket around himself.

4. The man is **dragged dragging** his right foot.

5. Stop **drum drumming** on the table.

Check your answers with the key on page 142.

F SUPPLEMENTARY WRITING EXERCISE

The ten new words that were taught in this lesson are:

arrange	blessing	clapping	date	dripping
forgotten	hugging	newspaper	spinning	wisdom

Choose any three of your new words from the box and write them in sentences.

1. _____

2. _____

3. _____

Look at the words in the column at the right. Choose the correct word and write it in the blank to best complete the sentence.

Check and Write

1. Bruce's leg was _____ after his fall. bubbly bloody cloudy

2. Lois plays _____ every day after school. outdoors peddler rooster

3. Will you _____ your candy with me? swallow struggle share

4. You must be _____ when someone is talking. stupid thirsty silent

5. My _____ dog could hardly keep his head up. juicy sleepy steamy

6. When you get to my house, _____ on the window. press lean tap

7. After I eat ice cream, I am always _____. puffy glittery thirsty

8. I like to stay in my _____ bed on cold mornings. meaty toasty cloudy

9. That man is a _____ to America. visitor fisherman butterfly

10. A _____ wakes me every morning at six. coward woodpecker fiddle

11. It is fun to _____ good books with my friends. share prove shed

12. When it is my turn to play, _____ me on the back. sweep whip tap

13. I am always polite when a _____ comes to our house. passenger kangaroo visitor

14. The _____ cat drank all its cream. thirsty steamy rubbery

15. Did you ever see a _____ movie? sudden silent weak

16. In summer, we cook _____. outdoors paste wool

17. The room became _____ after I started a fire. scratchy puffy toasty

18. A _____ digs in the tree near my house. giant woodpecker knight

19. I suddenly became very _____. sleepy speedy soapy

20. Ken's arm was scratched and now his shirt is _____. stuffy cloudy bloody

_____.

bloody (blud'ē), **1.** bleeding: *a bloody nose.* **2.** accompanied by much killing: *It was a bloody battle.* **3.** eager to kill. **4.** to stain with blood. *adj.,* **blood i er, blood i est,** *v.,* **blood ied, blood y ing.**

share (shār), **1.** part; portion; part belonging to one individual: *Dan does more than his share of the work.* **2.** each of the parts into which the ownership of a company or corporation is divided: *The ownership of this railroad is divided into several million shares.* **3.** divide into parts, each taking a part: *The knight shared his bread with the beggar.* **4.** use together; enjoy together; have in common: *The sisters share the same room.* **5.** have a share; take part: *Everyone shared in making the party a success.* *n., v.,* **shared, shar ing.**

si lent (sī'lənt), **1.** not speaking; saying little or nothing: *The stranger was silent about his early life. Pupils must be silent during the study hour.* **2.** quiet; still; noiseless: *a silent house.* **3.** not spoken; not said out loud: *a silent prayer. The "e" in "time" is a silent letter.* **4.** taking no open or active part. A silent partner has no share in managing a business. *adj.*

sleepy (slēp'ē), **1.** ready to go to sleep; inclined to sleep. **2.** quiet; not active. *adj.,* **sleep i er, sleep i est.**

tap (tap), **1.** strike lightly: *He tapped on the floor with his foot.* **2.** light blow: *There was a tap at the door.* **3.** make, put, etc., by light blows: *to tap a message.* *v.,* **tapped, tap ping,** *n.*

thirsty (thėrs'tē), **1.** feeling thirst; having thirst: *The dog is thirsty; please give him some water.* **2.** without water or moisture; dry. *adj.,* **thirst i er, thirst i est.**

toast (tōst), **1.** slices of bread browned by heat. **2.** brown by heat: *We toasted the bread.* **3.** heat thoroughly: *He toasted his feet before the open fire.* **4.** propose as a toast; drink to the health of: *The men toasted the general.* *n., v.*

B   USING CONTEXT CLUES

Place an X in front of each correct answer. The word may be used correctly in one or both of the sentences.

1. If Tony and his brother <u>shared</u> a room,
   ____ a. they used it together.
   ____ b. they used only one-half of it.

2. If Jason <u>toasted</u> the bread,
   ____ a. he heated it.
   ____ b. he browned it.

3. Which of the following sentences uses the underlined word correctly?
   ____ a. The <u>sleepy</u> child couldn't keep his eyes open.
   ____ b. It is a quiet, <u>sleepy</u> day.

4. Which of the following sentences uses the underlined word correctly?
   ____ a. The <u>thirsty</u> earth drank up the water.
   ____ b. He is over <u>thirsty</u> years old.

5. Which of the following sentences uses the underlined word correctly?
   ____ a. After the car crash, two people were <u>bloody</u>.
   ____ b. A <u>bloody</u> cut should be cleaned carefully.

Check your answers with the key on page 142.

C CHECKING THE MEANING

Read the words in the boxes. Choose the word that best completes the sentence under them. Write that word on the line. Then complete the next sentence by placing an X in front of the correct answer.

1. | silent | | silently |

   Why are you so _____ about what you did today?
   The word you wrote means
   ____ a. unhappy.
   ____ b. quiet.
   ____ c. pleased.

2. | share | | shared |

   Dotty _____ her sandwich with Stuart.
   The word you wrote means
   ____ a. a part of something.
   ____ b. take part in something.
   ____ c. broke into parts, each taking a part.

3. | toast | | toasted |

   Every night I _____ my back near the fire.
   From this sentence, you know that
   ____ a. I try to get my back brown.
   ____ b. I get my back warm.
   ____ c. I drink by the fire.

4. | tapped | | tapping |

   Billy _____ me on the head.
   The word you wrote means
   ____ a. struck lightly.
   ____ b. a light blow.
   ____ c. make by hitting.

5. | bloodiest | | bloody |

   A car hit our dog and made it _____ .
   From this sentence, you know that
   ____ a. our dog will get better.
   ____ b. our dog was hurt.
   ____ c. a car tried to kill our dog.

Check your answers with the key on page 142.

67

D   COMPLETING THE SENTENCES

Choose a word from the box that best completes each sentence. Write it on the line.

blood	luck	sleep	thirst	toast
or	*or*	*or*	*or*	*or*
bloody	lucky	sleepy	thirsty	toasty

1. With just a little _____, I may get a job tomorrow.

2. Did you _____ long enough last night?

3. Terry's arm was _____ after the crash.

4. I have two pieces of _____ every morning.

5. I'm so _____, I would drink anything.

Check your answers with the key on page 142.

E   USING THE SKILL

Underline the word that best completes each sentence.

1. This engine runs on **steam steamy**.

2. Squirrels have **bush bushy** tails.

3. Marty cannot wear anything made from **wool wooly**.

4. We used **oil oily** to stop the door's squeaking.

5. The **rain rainy** will help the flowers grow.

Check your answers with the key on page 142.

F   SUPPLEMENTARY WRITING EXERCISE

The ten new words that were taught in this lesson are:

bloody	outdoors	share	silent	sleepy
tap	thirsty	toasty	visitor	woodpecker

Choose any three of your new words from the box and write them in sentences.

1. _____

2. _____

3. _____

Look at the words in the column at the right. Choose the correct word and write it in the blank to best complete the sentence.

Check and Write

1. My dog does tricks to _____ me.

amuse   enjoy   fear

2. I have been _____ too much money.

boasting   allowing   borrowing

3. Do you think you will win the art _____?

contest   feast   signal

4. The _____ of my hat was all pushed in.

thread   stump   crown

5. The motor of the car is covered with _____.

paste   grease   ribbon

6. To be _____, you must take care of yourself.

healthy   bloody   cloudy

7. The horse was _____ to jump over the fence.

announcing   refusing   behaving

8. Gold is very _____ these days.

comfortable   fresh   scarce

9. Herb was too _____ to wear his old clothes.

stout   healthy   gentle

10. Were you _____ when I was late?

dirtied   skinny   worried

11. The dog was _____ to eat its food.

staring   refusing   rattling

12. I plan to enter the writing _____.

contest   plane   tribe

13. On rainy days, I _____ myself by reading.

unite   invite   amuse

14. My grandmother may be old, but she is very

_____.

toasty   healthy   salty

15. Don't slip on the _____ on the floor.

path   mice   grease

16. Peter was _____, but he could run very fast.

polite   stout   mad

17. I get very _____ before a test.

worried   simple   shady

18. In the school play I wore a _____ on my head.

robe   pole   crown

19. Food is _____ in many parts of the world.

scarce   possible   known

20. Caroline is always _____ my books.

guarding   borrowing   wasting

amuse (ə mūz'), **1.** entertain; turn to pleasant thoughts and feelings; cause to feel cheerful and happy: *The sailor amused the little boy by telling him a story.* **2.** cause to laugh or smile, *v.,* **amused, amus ing.**

con test (kon'test for *n.,* kən test' for *v.*), **1.** a trial of skill. A game or race is a contest. **2.** dispute; struggle; fight. **3.** try to win. **4.** fight for; struggle for: *The soldiers contested every inch of ground. n., v.*

crown (kroun), **1.** head covering for a king or queen. **2.** royal power; supreme governing power in a monarchy. **The Crown** granted lands in America to certain men. **3.** make king, queen, etc. **4.** of a crown; having to do with a crown: *crown jewels.* **5.** to honor; reward: *His work was crowned with success.* **6.** head. **7.** top part: *the crown of a hat, the crown of a mountain.* **8.** part of a tooth which appears beyond the gum, or an artificial substitute for it. *n., v., adj.*

King wearing a crown

re fuse (ri fūz'), **1.** say "no" to: *He refuses the offer. She refused him when he begged her to marry him.* **2.** say one will not do it, give it, etc.: *He refuses to obey. v.,* **re fused, re fus ing.**

scarce (skãrs), **1.** hard to get; rare: *Good cooks are scarce. Very old stamps are scarce.* **2.** scarcely. **3. Make oneself scarce** means (1) go away. (2) stay away. [Used in common talk] *adj.,* **scarc er, scarc est, adv.**

stout (stout), **1.** fat and large. **2.** firm; strong; strongly built: *The fort has stout walls.* **3.** brave; bold. **4.** a dark-brown beer. *adj., n.*

wor ry (wėr'ē), **1.** feel anxious; be uneasy: *She worries about little things.* **2.** bother; annoy; vex; trouble: *Don't worry your father with so many questions.* **3.** care; anxiety; uneasiness; trouble. **4.** seize and shake with the teeth; bite at; snap at: *The dog worried the rat. v.,* **wor ried, wor ry ing, n., pl.** **wor ries.**

B   USING CONTEXT CLUES

Place an X in front of each correct answer. The word may be used correctly in one or both of the sentences.

1. If Art worried his friends,
   ____ a.   his friends were uneasy.
   ____ b.   he bit his friends.

2. If Elizabeth was crowned Queen of England,
   ____ a.   she was made queen.
   ____ b.   she was rewarded.

3. If a fight was won by the stoutest men,
   ____ a.   the men were fat.
   ____ b.   the men were drinking beer.

4. If Dave contested his telephone bill,
   ____ a.   he won a month of free telephone use.
   ____ b.   he was fighting the bill for some reason.

5. Which of the following sentences uses the underlined word correctly?
   ____ a.   Frank amused the job he was offered.
   ____ b.   The puppy amused the baby for a short time.

Check your answers with the key on page 142.

| C | CHECKING THE MEANING |

Read the words in the boxes. Choose the word that best completes the sentence under them. Write that word on the line. Then complete the next sentence by placing an X in front of the correct answer.

1. | crown | | crowning |

   The mountain's _____ was covered with snow.
   The word you wrote means
   ____ a.   part of a tooth.
   ____ b.   side.
   ____ c.   top part.

2. | scarce | | scarcer |

   "Make yourself _____," said the angry boy.
   From this sentence, you know that
   ____ a.   the boy was playing hard to get.
   ____ b.   the boy wanted someone to go away.
   ____ c.   the boy wanted something few people have.

3. | worried | | worry |

   The little dog is _____ because of the lion.
   The word you wrote means
   ____ a.   uneasy.
   ____ b.   careful.
   ____ c.   pleased.

4. | crown | | crowned |

   Jack fell down and broke his _____.
   From this sentence, you know that
   ____ a.   Jack broke his power.
   ____ b.   Jack broke his head.
   ____ c.   Jack got a reward.

5. | contested | | contesting |

   Brenda is _____ her right to live away from home.
   The word you wrote means
   ____ a.   fighting for.
   ____ b.   fighting against.
   ____ c.   a game or race.

Check your answers with the key on page 142.

D	COMPLETING THE SENTENCES

Choose a word from the box that best completes each sentence. Write it on the line.

amuse	borrow	health	refuse	worry
or	*or*	*or*	*or*	*or*
amusing	borrowing	healthy	refusing	worried

1. May I _____ your bicycle?

2. I am reading a very _____ book.

3. Mr. Trotta is _____ about his daughter.

4. Will you _____ to buy a gift for Sidney?

5. How has your _____ been these past few days?

Check your answers with the key on page 142.

E	USING THE SKILL

Underline the word that best completes each sentence.

1. Terry **tried try** reading that book, but she didn't like it.

2. What's that **floated floating** in the water?

3. The mouse **nibbled nibbling** at the cheese.

4. The children all started **tooted tooting** horns at the same time.

5. This ice cream is rich and **cream creamy**.

Check your answers with the key on page 142.

F	SUPPLEMENTARY WRITING EXERCISE

The ten new words that were taught in this lesson are:

amuse	borrowing	contest	crown	grease
healthy	refusing	scarce	stout	worried

Choose any three of your new words from the box and write them in sentences.

1. _____

2. _____

3. _____

A LEARNING THE WORDS

Look at the words in the column at the right. Choose the correct word and write it in the blank to best complete the sentence.

Check and Write

1. A _____ of wind sent the leaves flying.

    shot   grain   blast

2. It is usually _____ before a storm.

    pale   calm   cozy

3. I have _____ one dollar in my pocket.

    blindly   calmly   exactly

4. I always try to act _____.

    politely   carelessly   deadly

5. The airplane landed _____.

    eagerly   faintly   safely

6. Marcia's illness is not very _____.

    heavenly   serious   orderly

7. The snow fell _____ to the ground.

    silently   plainly   politely

8. Jerry always speaks _____.

    costly   richly   softly

9. I was _____ by the barking dog.

    startled   refused   crowned

10. There is a lot of _____ on the roads today.

    coffee   dust   traffic

11. Try to do _____ as I do.

    neatly   blindly   exactly

12. I want to talk about something very _____.

    complete   serious   average

13. The plane took off with a big _____.

    blast   dash   beat

14. The cat walked _____ across the room.

    loosely   silently   heavenly

15. Jack _____ held the door open.

    politely   fiercely   madly

16. It is dangerous to play in _____.

    palaces   traffic   bedrooms

17. You should always pet an animal _____.

    boldly   clearly   softly

18. Peter reached home _____.

    safely   freely   completely

19. I was _____ when the balloon broke.

    corrected   startled   divided

20. Try to be _____ when other people are excited.

    calm   fancy   eager

blast (blast), **1.** strong sudden rush of wind or air: *the icy blasts of winter.* **2.** the sound made by blowing a horn or trumpet. **3.** blow up (rocks, earth, etc.) by dynamite, etc.: *The old building was blasted.* **4.** explosion: *We heard the blast a mile away. n., v.*

calm (käm), **1.** quiet; still; not stormy or windy; not stirred up; peaceful: *a calm sea, a calm voice.* **2.** quietness; stillness; absence of wind or motion. **3.** make calm; become calm: *Mother soon calmed the baby. The baby calmed down. adj., n., v.*

po lite (pə līt), **1.** behaving properly; having or showing good manners. **2.** refined; elegant. *Helen wished to learn all the customs of polite society. adj.*

se ri ous (sir'ē ə s), **1.** thoughtful; grave: *a serious face.* **2.** in earnest; not fooling: *Are you joking or serious?* **3.** important; needing thought: *Raising money for our club is a serious matter.* **4.** important because it may do much harm; dangerous: *The badly injured man was in a serious condition. adj.*

soft (sôft), **1.** not hard; not stiff; yielding easily to touch: *Feathers, cotton, and wool are soft.* **2.** not hard compared with other things of the same sort: *Pine is softer than oak. Marble is softer stone than granite.* **3.** smooth; pleasant to the touch; not rough or coarse: *the soft hair of a kitten, soft silk.* **4.** quietly pleasant; mild: *a soft spring morning, soft air, soft words, the soft light of candles.* **5.** gentle; kind; tender: *soft voice, soft eyes, soft heart.* **6.** weak: *The army had become soft from idleness and luxury.* **7. Soft drinks** are drinks that do not contain alcohol. **8. Soft water** is water that is easy to wash with. *adj., adv.*

traf fic (traf'ik), **1.** people, automobiles, wagons, ships, etc., coming and going along a way of travel: *Police control the traffic in large cities.* **2.** buy; sell; exchange; carry on trade: *The men trafficked with the natives for ivory. n., v.,* **traf ficked, traf fick ing.**

B   USING CONTEXT CLUES

Place an X in front of each correct answer. The word may be used correctly in one or both of the sentences.

1. If James was <u>trafficking</u> cars,
    - ＿＿ a. he was buying and selling them.
    - ＿＿ b. he was doing a lot of traveling.

2. If Tina's voice <u>quieted</u> the animal,
    - ＿＿ a. she made the animal calm.
    - ＿＿ b. she made the animal excited.

3. Which of the following sentences uses the underlined word correctly?
    - ＿＿ a. A <u>blast</u> of cold air came through the open window.
    - ＿＿ b. The boy <u>blasted</u> the balloon.

4. If Martha was <u>seriously</u> thinking about leaving her job,
    - ＿＿ a. she wanted a new job.
    - ＿＿ b. she was thinking carefully.

5. Which of the following sentences uses the underlined word correctly?
    - ＿＿ a. We serve only <u>soft</u> drinks here.
    - ＿＿ b. Silver is <u>softer</u> than gold.

Check your answers with the key on page 143.

C   CHECKING THE MEANING

Read the words in the boxes. Choose the word that best completes the sentence under them. Write that word on the line. Then complete the next sentence by placing an X in front of the correct answer.

1. | soft | | softly |

   Vera has a _____ spot in her heart for animals.
   From this sentence, you know that
   ____ a.   Vera likes to touch animals.
   ____ b.   Vera does not like animals.
   ____ c.   Vera likes all kinds of animals.

2. | serious | | seriously |

   The man was not _____ hurt.
   From this sentence, you know that
   ____ a.   the man died.
   ____ b.   the man was very sick.
   ____ c.   the man would be all right.

3. | blast | | blasted |

   Tammy gave one loud _____ on her horn.
   The word you wrote means
   ____ a.   a rush of air.
   ____ b.   a sound.
   ____ c.   blow up.

4. | calm | | calmly |

   It was strangely _____ in the zoo today.
   From this sentence, you know that
   ____ a.   it was very quiet.
   ____ b.   there were no people around.
   ____ c.   nothing moved.

5. | traffic | | trafficked |

   There is not much _____ in the city on Sunday.
   The word you wrote means
   ____ a.   buying.
   ____ b.   selling.
   ____ c.   traveling.

Check your answers with the key on page 143.

D COMPLETING THE SENTENCES

Choose a word from the box that best completes each sentence. Write it on the line.

calm	exact	polite	silent	soft
or	*or*	*or*	*or*	*or*
calmly	exactly	politely	silently	softly

1. Mary sang so _____ to her baby that we could not hear her.

2. Ellen _____ gave her seat to the old man.

3. This is _____ how I want it done.

4. The house was _____ after everyone went to sleep.

5. When the eye of the storm passed overhead, all was _____.

Check your answers with the key on page 143.

E USING THE SKILL

Underline the word that best completes each sentence.

1. Are you **certain certainly** that Jane left at eight?

2. Mark **usual usually** comes home right after school.

3. The squirrel **quick quickly** ran up the tree.

4. You must be very **proud proudly** of your son.

5. Phyllis is home **sick sickly**.

Check your answers with the key on page 143.

F SUPPLEMENTARY WRITING EXERCISE

The ten new words that were taught in this lesson are:

blast	calm	exactly	politely	safely
serious	silently	softly	startled	traffic

Choose any three of your new words from the box and write them in sentences.

1. _____

2. _____

3. _____

A   LEARNING THE WORDS

Look at the words in the column at the right. Choose the correct word and write it in the blank to best complete the sentence.

Check and Write

1. Mother bought a used _____.

| desert | bulb | automobile |

2. John is the biggest _____ I ever met.

| loader | boaster | shooter |

3. The lamp _____ when it fell to the floor.

| dried | escaped | broke |

4. Christopher Columbus was the _____ of America.

| discoverer | coaster | complainer |

5. He is an _____ of fine music.

| ironer | enjoyer | offerer |

6. Why do you always have a _____ on your face?

| frown | growl | hug |

7. The setting sun was _____ by the clouds.

| planned | worn | hidden |

8. The _____ are looking for the thief.

| police | woman | eagles |

9. A _____ broke into our house.

| bather | dreamer | robber |

10. What is the _____ going to talk about?

| speaker | drifter | floater |

11. I _____ when I am unhappy.

| practice | frown | wink |

12. The baby's toy _____ when he threw it down.

| stretched | formed | broke |

13. The _____ in this city are kept very busy.

| knights | police | eagles |

14. Who won the _____ race?

| carrot | banana | automobile |

15. Last night's _____ talked about how to get a job.

| speaker | moaner | repeater |

16. Charles was _____ by the tall tree.

| disappointed | hidden | worn |

17. Most people don't like a _____.

| boaster | marcher | mixer |

18. "What did the _____ take?" asked the policeman.

| earner | learner | robber |

19. Are you an _____ of good books?

| ironer | enjoyer | alarmer |

20. The _____ of that gold mine became famous.

| discoverer | packer | pretender |

boast (bōst), 1. speak too highly of oneself; praise what one is or does. 2. a statement in praise of oneself. 3. something that one is proud of. 4. be proud of. 5. have (something) to be proud of: *Our town boasts a new school.* *v., n.*

break (brāk), 1. make come to pieces by a blow or pull: *Baby has broken her doll.* 2. come apart; crack; burst: *The plate broke into pieces when it fell on the floor.* 3. fail to keep; act against: *He never breaks a promise. People who break the law are punished.* 4. force a way: *The man broke loose from prison. A thief broke into the house.* 5. dig or plow (the ground). 6. stop; put an end to: *to break one's fast.* 7. lessen the force of: *The wind is broken by the trees* 8. make known; reveal: *Some one must break the news of the boy's accident to his mother.* 9. train to obey; tame: *to break a colt, to break a person's spirit.* 10. come suddenly: *War broke out. The storm broke within ten minutes.* 11. fail; become weak; give way: *The dog's heart broke when his master died.* 12. dawn; appear: *The day is breaking.* 13. go beyond: *The speed of the new train has broken all records.* 14. a short interruption in work, practice, etc.: *The coach told us to take a break for five minutes.* *v.,* broke, bro ken, break ing, *n.*

hide (hīd), 1. put out of sight; keep out of sight: *Hide it where no one else will know of it or know where it is.* 2. shut off from sight; be in front of: *Clouds hide the sun.* 3. keep secret: *Mary hid her disappointment.* 4. hide oneself: *I'll hide and you find me.* *v.,* hid, hid den or hid, hid ing.

po lice (pə lēs'), 1. the department of government that keeps order and arrests persons who break the law. 2. the men who do this for a city or state. 3. keep in order: *to police the camp.* *n., v.* po liced, po lic ing.

speak (spēk), 1. say words; talk: *A cat cannot speak. Speak distinctly.* 2. make a speech: *John spoke for the group that wanted a picnic.* 3. say; tell; express; make known: *Speak the truth.* 4. use (a language): *Do you speak French?* 5. Speak out or speak up means speak loudly, clearly, or freely. 6. So to speak means to speak in such a manner. *v.,* spoke, spo ken, speak ing.

speaker (spēk'ər), 1. person who speaks. 2. the presiding officer. *n.*

B   USING CONTEXT CLUES

Place an X in front of each correct answer. The word may be used correctly in one or both of the sentences.

1. If five men are policing their apartment house,
   _____ a.   they are joining the police.
   _____ b.   they are making sure nothing is wrong.

2. If John boasts about his new school,
   _____ a.   he is proud of his school.
   _____ b.   he doesn't like his school.

3. If the baby is just learning to speak,
   _____ a.   he is talking English.
   _____ b.   he is saying words.

4. Which of the following sentences uses the underlined word correctly?
   _____ a.   The horse broke away from the man.
   _____ b.   Take a ten minute break.

5. Which of the following sentences uses the underlined word correctly?
   _____ a.   Where did you hide my keys?
   _____ b.   The clouds hidden the rain.

Check your answers with the key on page 143.

C CHECKING THE MEANING

Read the words in the boxes. Choose the word that best completes the sentence under them. Write that word on the line. Then complete the next sentence by placing an X in front of the correct answer.

1. | boast | | boaster |

That was some _____ Jim just made!
From this sentence, you know that
____ a. Jim is proud of something.
____ b. Jim spoke too highly about something.
____ c. Jim has something to be proud of.

2. | police | | policing |

There is a dog _____ this store every night.
From this sentence, you know that
____ a. the dog belongs to a policeman.
____ b. the dog is a police dog.
____ c. the dog is watching the store.

3. | speaking | | spoke |

I didn't know Tina _____ only French to her grandmother.
From this sentence, you know that
____ a. Tina can say a few words in French.
____ b. Tina can use French very well.
____ c. Tina was talking about French.

4. | break | | broken |

Nan hopes to _____ the world's swimming record.
The word you wrote means
____ a. to make something come apart.
____ b. to go beyond.
____ c. to put an end to.

5. | broke | | broken |

We _____ for lunch at noon.
The word you wrote means
____ a. to stop doing something.
____ b. to come suddenly.
____ c. to act against.

Check your answers with the key on page 143.

79

D   COMPLETING THE SENTENCES

Choose a word from the box that best completes each sentence. Write it on the line.

boast	discover	enjoy	rob	speak
or	*or*	*or*	*or*	*or*
boaster	discoverer	enjoyer	robber	speaker

1. Did you _____ your night out?

2. The _____ took my watch and ring.

3. At what time will the _____ begin his talk?

4. When did you _____ that your book was missing?

5. That was the biggest _____ Jason ever made.

Check your answers with the key on page 143.

E   USING THE SKILL

Underline the word that best completes each sentence.

1. I'm just a **wander wanderer** going from town to town.

2. Have you ever seen your name in **print printer**?

3. Please **sweep sweeper** the floor.

4. Chuck is the best **bowl bowler** I know.

5. What song do you want to **sing singer**?

Check your answers with the key on page 143.

F   SUPPLEMENTARY WRITING EXERCISE

The ten new words that were taught in this lesson are:

| automobile | boaster | broke | discoverer | enjoyer |
| frown | hidden | police | robber | speaker |

Choose any three of your new words from the box and write them in sentences.

1. _____

2. _____

3. _____

A   LEARNING THE WORDS

Look at the words in the column at the right. Choose the correct word and write it in the blank to best complete the sentence.

Check and Write

1. My mother gets angry when I do not _____.   behave   travel   shake

2. Give me an _____ of what you mean.   excuse   example   exercise

3. Sir Kay was a _____ of the Round Table.   knight   knife   stealer

4. After the fire, we had to _____ our house.   restuff   rebuild   refreeze

5. John will _____ in a year.   recharge   reload   remarry

6. I hope to _____ this book soon.   reunite   retest   reread

7. Would you _____ what you just said?   recopy   restate   respray

8. Don't _____ the dog so tightly.   squeeze   trap   harm

9. That dog will _____ any chance he gets.   sting   slip   stray

10. My brother has a very quick _____ .   grain   temper   force

11. Parents must set a good _____ for their children.   example   average   direction

12. Did you _____ that story yet?   refreeze   reread   rewrap

13. My sister brought home a _____ dog.   stray   narrow   free

14. Butch can _____ through that hole in the fence.   pitch   gather   squeeze

15. Can you _____ the doghouse with that wood?   resweep   rebuild   rethread

16. Do you think Sonia will ever _____?   remarry   rebuild   reshape

17. I hope the children will _____ nicely.   nibble   struggle   behave

18. I will _____ exactly how I feel.   rearrange   restate   recorrect

19. Have you ever wished you were a brave _____?   knight   visitor   giant

20. Sometimes I lose my _____ too fast.   straw   treasure   temper

ex am ple (eg zam′pl), **1.** a sample; one thing taken to show what the others are like: *New York is an example of a busy seaport.* **2.** a model; a pattern: *Lincoln is a good example for boys to follow.* **Set an example** means give, show, or be an example. **3.** a problem in arithmetic. **4.** warning to others: *The captain made an example of the soldiers who shirked by making them clean up the camp. n.*

read (rēd), **1.** get the meaning of writing or print: *We read books.* **2.** speak out loud the words of writing or print: *Please read it to me.* **3.** study: *David is reading law.* **4.** show by figures, letters, signs, etc.: *The thermometer reads 70 degrees. The ticket reads "From New York to Boston."* **5.** give the meaning of; interpret: *Silence is not always to be read as consent.* **Read between the lines** means find a meaning not actually expressed in the writing or print. *v.,* **read** (red), **read ing.**

squeeze (skwēz), **1.** press hard: *Don't squeeze the kitten; you will hurt it.* **2.** force by pressing: *I can't squeeze another thing into my trunk.* **3.** hug. **4.** crush; crowd: *It's a tight squeeze to get five people in that little car.* **5.** force a way: *He squeezed through the crowd. v.,* **squeezed, squeez ing,** *n.*

state (stāt), **1.** condition of a person or thing: *He is in a poor state of health. The house is in a bad state of repair.* **2.** nation. **3.** one of several organized political groups of people which together form a nation: *The State of Texas is one of the United States.* **4.** tell in speech or writing: *State your opinion of the new school rules.* **5.** the structure or form of a material: *A material may exist in a solid, liquid, or gaseous state. n., v.,* **stat ed, stat ing,** *adj.*

stray (strā), **1.** wander; roam; lose one's way: *Our dog has strayed off somewhere.* **2.** wandering; lost: *A stray cat is crying at the door.* **3.** wanderer; lost animal. **4.** scattered; here and there: *There were a few stray fishermen's huts along the beach. v., adj., n.*

tem per (tem′pər), **1.** state of mind; disposition; condition: *She has a sweet temper. He flies into a temper at trifles. He became angry and lost his temper.* **2.** moderate; soften: *Temper justice with mercy.* **3.** bring to a proper or desired condition by mixing or preparing. A painter tempers his colors by mixing them with oil. **4.** the hardness, toughness, etc., of the mixture: *The temper of the clay was right for shaping. n., v.*

B USING CONTEXT CLUES

Place an X *in front of each correct answer. The word may be used correctly in one or both of the sentences.*

1. Which of the following sentences uses the underlined word correctly?
   ____ a. Agnes <u>tempered</u> the paint before she started to work.
   ____ b. Mr. Ricco lost his <u>temper</u> when his son was late.

2. If Sam <u>squeezed</u> one more shirt into his case,
   ____ a. he forced it in.
   ____ b. he hugged it.

3. Which of the following sentences uses the underlined word correctly?
   ____ a. I have ten <u>examples</u> to do.
   ____ b. Tom made an <u>example</u> out of his boat.

4. Which of the following sentences uses the underlined word correctly?
   ____ a. Monica <u>read</u> between the lines of her son's letter.
   ____ b. Herbie is <u>reading</u> a story to Casey.

5. If Linda didn't like Jack's <u>state</u>,
   ____ a. Linda didn't like where Jack lived.
   ____ b. Linda thought something was wrong with Jack.

Check your answers with the key on page 143.

C CHECKING THE MEANING

Read the words in the boxes. Choose the word that best completes the sentence under them. Write that word on the line. Then complete the next sentence by placing an X in front of the correct answer.

1. | read |　| reading |

   George is _____ history.
   The word you wrote means
   ____ a. explaining.
   ____ b. studying.
   ____ c. showing

2. | stray |　| strayed |

   There were a few _____ books left in the old house.
   The word you wrote means
   ____ a. scattered.
   ____ b. wandering.
   ____ c. old and torn.

3. | temper |　| tempered |

   That horse has a mean _____.
   The word you wrote means
   ____ a. state of mind.
   ____ b. soft.
   ____ c. mix.

4. | example |　| examples |

   That drawing is a good _____ of the painter's work.
   From this sentence, you know that
   ____ a. the drawing is a warning.
   ____ b. everyone likes the drawing.
   ____ c. the drawing is a model of the painter's best work.

5. | squeezed |　| squeezing |

   Lois _____ Jim's hand as hard as she could.
   The word you wrote means
   ____ a. pressed hard.
   ____ b. hugged.
   ____ c. forced.

Check your answers with the key on page 143.

D COMPLETING THE SENTENCES

Choose a word from the box that best completes each sentence. Write it on the line.

build	marry	read	state	wrap
or	*or*	*or*	*or*	*or*
rebuild	remarry	reread	restate	rewrap

1. The Wilsons plan to _____ a new house.

2. Please _____ this package with that paper.

3. Janie did not wish to _____ after her husband died.

4. Mario _____ his wife's letter many times.

5. We didn't hear your question, so please _____ it.

Check your answers with the key on page 143.

E USING THE SKILL

Underline the word that best completes each sentence.

1. Jack lost his homework and had to **do redo** it.
2. Lily will **make remake** a cake today.
3. The box was packed so badly that we had to **load reload** it.
4. Where will you **restore store** these extra glasses?
5. When you **finish refinish** dinner, please wash the dishes.

Check your answers with the key on page 143.

F SUPPLEMENTARY WRITING EXERCISE

The ten new words that were taught in this lesson are:

behave	example	knight	rebuild	remarry
reread	restate	squeeze	stray	temper

Choose any three of your new words from the box and write them in sentences.

1. _____

2. _____

3. _____

A LEARNING THE WORDS	

Look at the words in the column at the right. Choose the correct word and write it in the blank to best complete the sentence.

Check and Write

1. Is that the _____ answer?

correct   common   clear

2. I am _____ about Gene's trip.

careless   foolish   curious

3. Paula was born _____.

deaf   damp   fancy

4. We knew the man was _____, because he used sign language.

dirty   smooth   dumb

5. I want you to _____ down with your hand as hard as you can.

steer   press   squeak

6. Dave eats too _____.

rapidly   lovely   boldly

7. I felt very _____ at the party.

uncommon   unclear   uncomfortable

8. Do you _____ the bird cage every morning?

unthread   uncover   unstamp

9. Our dog left her puppies _____.

unguarded   unplanned   unprepared

10. It is not _____ for Bill to come home late.

unselfish   unusual   unpleasant

11. I hope you were not _____ in that bed.

unrattled   unpackaged   uncomfortable

12. Aren't you _____ about how the story ends?

curious   healthy   greedy

13. My old dog is becoming _____.

rich   deaf   hollow

14. The young boy was both deaf and _____.

plain   simple   dumb

15. This gold should never be left _____.

unguarded   unscattered   unbattered

16. I came as _____ as I could.

clearly   rapidly   sweetly

17. That is my _____ address.

correct   master   hidden

18. Nat's eyes are a most _____ color.

unselfish   unplanned   unusual

19. If you are warm, _____ yourself.

uncover   unbless   unannounce

20. I have to _____ my dress before I can wear it.

dip   press   fasten

85

cor rect (kə rekt′), **1.** true; right: *the correct answer.* **2.** agreeing with a good standard of taste; proper: *correct manners.* **3.** set right; mark the mistakes in; change to what is right: *Our teacher corrects our speech.* **4.** punish; set right by punishing; find fault with to improve. *adj., v.*

cu ri ous (kyūr′ē əs), **1.** eager to know: *Small children are very curious, and ask many questions.* **2.** strange; odd; unusual. *adj.*

dumb (dum), **1.** not able to speak: *dumb animals.* **2.** silent; not speaking. **3.** stupid; dull. *Used in common talk. adj.*

press (pres), **1.** use force or weight steadily in pushing; push: *Press the button to ring the bell. Press all the juice out.* **2.** make smooth; flatten: *You press clothes with an iron.* **3.** hug: *Mother pressed the baby to her.* **4.** urge; keep asking (somebody) earnestly: *We pressed our guest to stay longer.* **5.** urge onward; cause to hurry. **6.** compel; force: *The government pressed people into its service.* **7.** a machine for pressing: *a printing press, an ironing press.* **8.** the newspapers and the people who write for them: *Our school picnic was reported by the press. v., n.*

rap id (rap′id), **1.** very quick; swift: *a rapid walk.* **2. Rapids** are a part of a river where the water rushes very swiftly. *adj., n.*

un com for ta ble (un kumf′tə bl or un kum′fər tə bl), **1.** not comfortable. **2.** uneasy. **3.** disagreeable; causing discomfort. *adj.*

un cov er (un kuv′ər), **1.** remove the cover from. **2.** reveal; expose; make known. **3.** remove one's hat or cap. *v.*

un guard ed (un gär′did), **1.** not protected. **2.** careless. *adj.*

un u su al (un ū′zhŭ ə l), not in common use; not common; rare; beyond the ordinary. *adj.*

B   USING CONTEXT CLUES

Place an X in front of each correct answer. The word may be used correctly in one or both of the sentences.

1. If Kurt was <u>uncomfortable</u> in Doug's company,
   ____ a.   Kurt was uneasy.
   ____ b.   Kurt was making Doug uneasy.

2. If Betsy's head was <u>uncovered</u>,
   ____ a.   she was not wearing a hat.
   ____ b.   she took off her hat.

3. If Lee remained <u>dumb</u> all through the play,
   ____ a.   she did not move.
   ____ b.   she did not speak.

4. Which of the following sentences uses the underlined word correctly?
   ____ a.   We are <u>pressed</u> for time.
   ____ b.   Philip <u>pressed</u> me to stay another day.

5. If Daniel is going to <u>correct</u> his own work,
   ____ a.   he has not made any mistakes.
   ____ b.   he is going to fix his mistakes.

Check your answers with the key on page 144.

C CHECKING THE MEANING

Read the words in the boxes. Choose the word that best completes the sentence under them. Write that word on the line. Then complete the next sentence by placing an X in front of the correct answer.

1. | curious | | curiously |
   | --- | --- | --- |

   The ducks walking across the road made a _____ sight.
   The word you wrote means
   ___ a. funny.
   ___ b. eager to know.
   ___ c. strange.

2. | rapid | | rapids |
   | --- | --- | --- |

   I want to go down the _____ in a boat.
   The word you wrote means
   ___ a. very quick.
   ___ b. rushing.
   ___ c. rushing water of a river.

3. | pressed | | pressing |
   | --- | --- | --- |

   The little boy _____ the dog to him.
   The word you wrote means
   ___ a. forced.
   ___ b. hugged.
   ___ c. rushed.

4. | unusual | | usual |
   | --- | --- | --- |

   It is _____ for Joan not to call her mother every day.
   From this sentence, you know that
   ___ a. Joan calls her mother almost every day.
   ___ b. Joan does not call her mother on Sundays.
   ___ c. Joan's mother calls Joan every day.

5. | press | | pressing |
   | --- | --- | --- |

   The _____ talked with the President for an hour.
   The word you wrote means
   ___ a. an iron.
   ___ b. the people who write for newspapers.
   ___ c. a machine that prints newspapers.

Check your answers with the key on page 144.

87

D COMPLETING THE SENTENCES

Choose a word from the box that best completes each sentence. Write it on the line.

comfortable	cover	guarded	noticed	usual
or	*or*	*or*	*or*	*or*
uncomfortable	uncover	unguarded	unnoticed	unusual

1. That story has an _____ ending that surprised me.

2. Sit in this soft chair and make yourself _____.

3. I _____ that Fran was not at the party.

4. The President is _____ by special police at all times.

5. Pam used her coat as a _____.

Check your answers with the key on page 144.

E USING THE SKILL

Underline the word that best completes each sentence.

1. Annie is sick and **able unable** to leave her house.

2. Your friends are always **unwelcome welcome** at our house.

3. **Tie Untie** your shoes before you take them off.

4. Bruce was **sure unsure** of how to go, so he left without us.

5. Do not come to school **prepared unprepared**.

Check your answers with the key on page 144.

F SUPPLEMENTARY WRITING EXERCISE

The ten new words that were taught in this lesson are:

correct	curious	deaf	dumb	press
rapidly	uncomfortable	uncover	unguarded	unusual

Choose any three of your new words from the box and write them in sentences.

1. _____

2. _____

3. _____

Look at the words in the column at the right. Choose the correct word and write it in the blank to best complete the sentence.

Check and Write

1. This magic trick will _____ Bernie.

attack   amaze   excuse

2. When did Harvey grow a _____?

carrot   vegetable   beard

3. Edith was _____ after her long run.

breathless   tasteless   harmless

4. This _____ takes very good pictures.

necklace   jar   camera

5. Stan wants _____ for his birthday.

fog   jewelry   cardboard

6. Ann wore a gold _____.

necklace   blanket   flap

7. Jeff will _____ the picture on the wall.

offer   salt   paste

8. It is _____ for you to go out in this storm.

priceless   senseless   powerless

9. Mary's house is always _____.

spotless   harmless   bloodless

10. That ring Joe found is _____.

greaseless   worthless   cheerless

11. Philip used _____ to fix the book.

paste   brick   steam

12. My clean room will _____ Mother.

awaken   amaze   invite

13. I've never seen your shirts so _____.

spotless   bloodless   powerless

14. Do you really think these books are _____?

greaseless   dustless   worthless

15. Christopher has a very heavy _____.

pencil   lump   beard

16. Frank and Alice had a _____ fight.

cheerless   senseless   priceless

17. Do you like the _____ Joyce is wearing?

necklace   lumber   harness

18. Did you take any pictures with your _____?

canary   drawer   camera

19. What _____ should I wear with this dress?

jewelry   curtain   trousers

20. Troy ran into the house, _____.

childless   ageless   breathless

amaze (ə māz'), surprise greatly; strike with sudden wonder: *The boy who had seemed so stupid amazed us all by his fine examination. She was so amazed by the surprise party that she could not think of anything to say.* v., amazed, amaz ing.

beard (bird), 1. hair growing on a man's face. 2. something resembling or suggesting this. The chin tuft of a goat is a beard; so are the stiff hairs around the beak of a bird. 3. hairs on the heads of plants like oats, barley, and wheat. *n., v.*

breath less (breth'lis), 1. out of breath: *Running made hm breathless.* 2. unable to breathe because of fear, excitement, etc.: *The scene left Anne breathless.* 3. without breath; dead. *adj.*

cam era (kam'ər ə), a machine for taking photographs. *n.*

paste (pāst), 1. a mixture, such as flour and water boiled together, that will stick paper together. 2. to stick with paste. 3. a soft mixture: *fish paste. This pottery was made from a paste of clay and water.* 4. pie dough. 5. a hard glassy material used in making imitations of jewels. *n., v.,* past ed, past ing.

sense less (sens'lis), 1. unconscious: *A hard blow on the head knocked him senseless.* 2. stupid; foolish. *adj.*

worth less (werth'lis), without worth; good-for-nothing; useless: *Throw those worthless, broken toys away. Don't read that worthless book. adj.*

B   USING CONTEXT CLUES

Place an X in front of each correct answer. The word may be used correctly in one or both of the sentences.

1. If Julie faced the camera and smiled,
   ____ a.   someone was taking her picture.
   ____ b.   she was taking a picture of someone.

2. If Bill did a senseless thing,
   ____ a.   he did something without thinking.
   ____ b.   he hit someone on the head.

3. Which of the following sentences uses the underlined word correctly?
   ____ a.   The jewels on that necklace are just paste.
   ____ b.   Mix the flour with water until it forms a paste.

4. Which of the following sentences uses the underlined word correctly?
   ____ a.   That gold ring is far from worthless.
   ____ b.   This old paper is worthless.

5. If Ann was amazed to see her baby walk for the first time,
   ____ a.   she was greatly surprised.
   ____ b.   she thought it was something special.

Check your answers with the key on page 144.

C CHECKING THE MEANING

Read the words in the boxes. Choose the word that best completes the sentence under them. Write that word on the line. Then complete the next sentence by placing an X in front of the correct answer.

1. | beard | | beardless |

   My father's _____ is white.
   From this sentence, you know that
   ____ a. my father is an old man.
   ____ b. my father has black hair on his head.
   ____ c. my father has white hair around his mouth.

2. | breath | | breathless |

   As Amy watched the frightening movie, she became_____.
   From this sentence, you know that
   ____ a. Amy could not breathe because of a cold.
   ____ b. Amy could not breathe because she was afraid.
   ____ c. Amy could not breathe because she was dead.

3. | paste | | pasted |

   Fran will _____ some pictures in her book.
   The word you wrote means
   ____ a. a soft mixture.
   ____ b. to stick with paste.
   ____ c. something used in making fake jewels.

4. | necklace | | necklaces |

   Marie's _____ is five years old.
   The word you wrote means
   ____ a. something to keep the neck warm.
   ____ b. jewelry worn around the neck.
   ____ c. the part of a shirt that goes around the neck.

5. | sense | | senseless |

   John's answer was _____.
   The word you wrote means
   ____ a. foolish.
   ____ b. wise.
   ____ c. correct.

Check your answers with the key on page 144.

D COMPLETING THE SENTENCES

Choose a word from the box that best completes each sentence. Write it on the line.

beard	breath	sense	spot	worth
or	*or*	*or*	*or*	*or*
beardless	breathless	senseless	spotless	worthless

1. How much is this painting _____?

2. Bennie's _____ is so long it covers his tie.

3. It is _____ for you to spend so much money.

4. I was _____ after climbing all those stairs.

5. Mary's dog has a big black _____ on his back.

Check your answers with the key on page 144.

E USING THE SKILL

Underline the word that best completes each sentence.

1. It was very **care careless** of you to lose your keys.

2. There is not a **star starless** in the sky tonight.

3. I don't usually **tire tireless** this easily.

4. The queen's jewelry is **price priceless**.

5. My **tooth toothless** dog can't chew meat.

Check your answers with the key on page 144.

F SUPPLEMENTARY WRITING EXERCISE

The ten new words that were taught in this lesson are:

| amaze | beard | breathless | camera | jewelry |
| necklace | paste | senseless | spotless | worthless |

Choose any three of your new words from the box and write them in sentences.

1. _____

2. _____

3. _____

A LEARNING THE WORDS

Look at the words in the column at the right. Choose the correct word and write it in the blank to best complete the sentence.

Check and Write

1. Do you always wait for a _____ before you buy?

blessing   blossom   bargain

2. Was your new camera very _____?

costly   famous   disappointing

3. I _____ an answer to my question.

earn   built   deserve

4. I'm just a _____, going from town to town.

drifter   trotter   presser

5. Mr. Parkinson is worth a _____.

holiday   fortune   promise

6. The animals' _____ was ready to feed the lions.

kisser   borrower   keeper

7. Jason is the _____ for our baseball team.

pitcher   charger   fastener

8. When will you _____ the dish you broke?

replace   reward   respect

9. Autumn is the _____ I like the best.

signal   season   shadow

10. Frank left his work _____.

understood   usually   undone

11. Please _____ the pencils you borrowed.

rescue   replace   refuse

12. Helen would never leave anything _____.

undone   often   alike

13. The football _____ will soon be starting.

coast   crowd   season

14. Dennis filled the _____ with milk.

pitcher   airport   bubble

15. Kim made a _____ when she sold her house.

chuckle   dime   fortune

16. Wayne got a _____ when he bought that car.

bunch   bargain   barrel

17. The _____ of the building will fix the window.

keeper   wrecker   plower

18. I think I _____ to earn more money.

act   intend   deserve

19. The _____ stayed in town for only a few days.

duster   drifter   marcher

20. The car is too _____ for us to buy.

costly   oily   greasy

bar gain (bär′gən), **1.** an agreement to trade or exchange: *Will you take $5 for it? Then it's a bargain.* **2.** something offered for sale cheap or bought cheap. **3.** make a bargain; come to terms. **4.** try to get good terms: *She stood for ten minutes bargaining with the man for the vegetables.* **5. Bargain for** sometimes means expect or be prepared for: *It is raining, and that is more than I bargained for.* *n., v.*

cost ly (kôst′lē), **1.** of great value: *The queen had costly jewels.* **2.** costing much: *The fool made costly mistakes.* *adj.,* cost li er, cost li est.

drift (drift), **1.** be carried along by currents of air or water: *A raft drifts if it is not steered.* **2.** be carried along by circumstances: *Some people just drift through life.* **3.** meaning; direction of thought: *I caught the drift of his words.* **4.** snow, sand, etc., heaped up by the wind. *v., n.*

for tune (fôr′chən), **1.** great deal of money or property; riches; wealth: *Henry Ford made a fortune.* **2.** luck; chance; what happens: *Fortune was against us; we lost.* **3.** good luck; success; prosperity. **4.** Tell a person's fortune means tell what is going to happen to him. *n.*

pitch er¹ (pich′ər), **1.** a container made of china, glass, silver, etc., with a lip at one side and a handle at the other. Pitchers are used for holding and pouring out water, milk, etc. **2.** amount that a pitcher holds. *n.*

pitch er² (pich′ər), the player on a baseball team who throws the ball for the batter to hit. *n.*

sea son (sē′zn), **1.** The four seasons of the year are spring, summer, autumn, and winter. **2.** any period of time marked by something special: *the Christmas season, the harvest season.* **3.** improve the flavor of: *Season your egg with salt.* **4.** give interest or character to: *to season conversation with wit.* **5.** make or become fit for use by a period of keeping or treatment: *Wood is seasoned for building by drying and hardening it.* *n., v.*

B   USING CONTEXT CLUES

Place an X in front of each correct answer. The word may be used correctly in one or both of the sentences.

1. Which of the following sentences uses the underlined word correctly?
   - ____ a.   How long must we season this wood before we can burn it?
   - ____ b.   The holiday season is a time of joy.

2. Which of the following sentences uses the underlined word correctly?
   - ____ a.   Marty put a fortune into fixing his car.
   - ____ b.   Marilyn told Sharon's fortune.

3. If Sherry is bargaining for the price of the ring,
   - ____ a.   Sherry is agreeing to buy the ring.
   - ____ b.   Sherry is trying to agree on a price.

4. If David drank a pitcher of milk,
   - ____ a.   he finished the whole pitcher.
   - ____ b.   he threw out the milk.

5. Which of the following sentences uses the underlined word correctly?
   - ____ a.   The drift of snow was four feet high.
   - ____ b.   The snow drift over the car.

Check your answers with the key on page 144.

| C CHECKING THE MEANING |

Read the words in the boxes. Choose the word that best completes the sentence under them.
Write that word on the line. Then complete the next sentence by placing an X in front of the
correct answer.

1. | cost | | costly |

   Phil bought a _____ ring for his wife.
   The word you wrote means
   ____ a. of great worth.
   ____ b. without worth.
   ____ c. very beautiful.

2. | bargain | | bargained |

   All this good luck was more than I _____ for.
   The word you wrote means
   ____ a. bought.
   ____ b. sold.
   ____ c. expected.

3. | season | | seasoning |

   Steve was _____ the meat when I walked in.
   The word you wrote means
   ____ a. adding things to make the taste better.
   ____ b. making it interesting.
   ____ c. a special time.

4. | drift | | drifted |

   The boat _____ down the river.
   The word you wrote means
   ____ a. meaning.
   ____ b. was carried along.
   ____ c. piled up.

5. | pitcher | | pitchers |

   Theo did not like being _____.
   The word you wrote means
   ____ a. what a pitcher holds.
   ____ b. one who throws a ball.
   ____ c. something that holds liquids.

Check your answers with the key on page 144.

D   COMPLETING THE SENTENCES

Choose a word from the box that best completes each sentence. Write it on the line.

cost *or* costly	done *or* undone	drift *or* drifter	pitch *or* pitcher	place *or* replace

1. Please _____ this glass where it will be safe.

2. Fred has not _____ his homework.

3. Why do you always _____ from place to place?

4. How much did that book _____?

5. The _____ threw the ball to first base.

Check your answers with the key on page 144.

E   USING THE SKILL

Underline the word that best completes each sentence.

1. Did I answer that question **correct correctly**?

2. The **dive diver** swam under the water.

3. This house needs a new coat of **paint repaint**.

4. The fruit **spoiled unspoiled** from the heat.

5. Holidays should be full of **joy joyless**.

Check your answers with the key on page 144.

F   SUPPLEMENTARY WRITING EXERCISE

The ten new words that were taught in this lesson are:

bargain	costly	deserve	drifter	fortune
keeper	pitcher	replace	season	undone

Choose any three of your new words from the box and write them in sentences.

1. _____

2. _____

3. _____

Look at the words in the column at the right. Choose the correct word and write it in the blank to best complete the sentence.

Check and Write

1. I was _____ by what Loren told me.

arranged   attacked   astonished

2. I enjoy the _____ of a fresh snowfall.

blossom   beauty   batter

3. I think Charles is _____ than David.

braver   clearer   fainter

4. Put these things in that _____ box.

fresh   healthy   cardboard

5. Laura eats _____ every day for breakfast.

paste   cereal   rubber

6. Watch the bird _____ its wings as it flies.

flap   strike   freeze

7. The _____ are full of clouds today.

moments   heavens   sidewalks

8. Are your clothes _____ on you since you lost weight?

looser   lesser   lower

9. You will be _____ here than outdoors on this rainy day.

smarter   steeper   safer

10. These shirts I washed should be a lot _____.

whiter   gentler   scarcer

11. Gather up the dirt with a piece of _____.

ribbon   cloth   cardboard

12. Close the _____ on this box.

curtain   flap   flame

13. That horse is a real _____!

beauty   captain   model

14. Your car will be much _____ after you wash it.

looser   gentler   whiter

15. Your money will be much _____ in a bank.

paler   freer   safer

16. The _____ seemed to open when the rain came.

heavens   sheets   stems

17. Do you like fruit in your _____?

puzzle   cereal   pillow

18. I was _____ to learn that Pete was the winner.

astonished   averaged   attacked

19. Policemen are no _____ than firemen.

stranger   braver   clearer

20. After eating so much, I have to make my belt_____.

fiercer   paler   looser

_____.

beau ty (bū'tē), **1.** good looks. **2.** that which pleases in flowers, music, pictures, etc.: *There is beauty in a fine thought or act.* **3.** something beautiful. **4.** beautiful woman. *n., pl.* **beau ties.**

brave (brāv), **1.** without fear; having courage; showing courage: *brave knights.* **2.** meet without fear: *The soldiers braved much danger.* **3.** dare; defy: *He braved the king's anger.* **4.** a North American Indian warrior. *adj.,* **brav er, brav est,** *n., v.,* **braved, brav ing.**

flap (flap), **1.** strike noisily with something broad and loose: *The sail flapped.* **2.** a blow from something broad and loose: *a flap from a whale's tail.* **3.** move (wings) up and down; fly by flapping the wings. **4.** piece hanging or fastened at one edge only: *the flap of cloth over the opening to his pocket.* *v.,* **flapped, flap ping,** *n.*

heav en (hev'ən), **1.** place where God and His angels live. **2.** God; Providence: *It was the will of Heaven.* **3.** place or condition of greatest happiness. **4.** upper air in which clouds float, winds blow, and birds fly; the sky. We usually say heavens. **5.** For **heaven's sake** and **Good heavens** are exclamations expressing surprise or a protest. *n., interj.*

loose (lüs), **1.** not fastened: *a loose thread.* **2.** not tight: *loose clothing.* **3.** not bound together: *loose papers.* **4.** free; not shut in or up: *We leave the dog loose at night.* **5.** not strict, close, or exact: *a loose translation from another language.* **6.** careless about morals or conduct: *a loose character.* *adj.,* **loos er, loos est,** *v.,* **loosed, loos ing,** *adv.*

safe (sāf), **1.** free from harm or danger: *Keep money in a safe place.* **2.** not causing harm or danger: *Is it safe to leave the house unlocked?* **3.** careful: *a safe guess, a safe move.* **4.** a place or container for keeping things safe. *adj.,* **saf er, saf est,** *n.*

Safe (def. 5)

white (hwīt), **1.** the color of snow. **2.** having this color. **3.** pale: *Alice turned white with fear.* **4.** light-colored: *white meat.* **5.** a white person. *n., adj.,* **whit er, whit est.**

B USING CONTEXT CLUES

Place an X in front of each correct answer. The word may be used correctly in one or both of the sentences.

1. If Frank braved the storm, you know that
   ____ a. he stayed indoors where it was safe.
   ____ b. he went out into the storm.

2. Which of the following sentences uses the underlined word correctly?
   ____ a. I am afraid I may loose my way in the woods.
   ____ b. Your button is loose.

3. If Mrs. Peter's hair seemed to turn white overnight,
   ____ a. something frightened her.
   ____ b. her hair became the color of snow.

4. If Timothy had only one safe move in a game he was playing,
   ____ a. he would lose if he wasn't careful.
   ____ b. he wanted to keep the game free from harm.

5. Which of the following sentences uses the underlined word correctly?
   ____ a. The clouds are high in the heavens.
   ____ b. Good heavens, aren't you ready yet?

Check your answers with the key on page 145.

C   CHECKING THE MEANING

Read the words in the boxes. Choose the word that best completes the sentence under them. Write that word on the line. Then complete the next sentence by placing an X in front of the correct answer.

1. | safe | | safer |

   It is _____ to say that Steve will not be late.
   From this sentence, you know that
   ____ a.   Steve is usually late.
   ____ b.   Steve is almost never late.
   ____ c.   Steve is very careful about what he says.

2. | beauties | | beauty |

   This painting shows the great _____ of that woman.
   The word you wrote means
   ____ a.   good looks.
   ____ b.   make beautiful.
   ____ c.   beautiful woman.

3. | flapped | | flapping |

   The beaver _____ its broad, flat tail.
   The word you wrote means
   ____ a.   fastened.
   ____ b.   made a noise.
   ____ c.   tried to fly.

4. | loose | | looser |

   The dog got _____ and ran away.
   The word you wrote means
   ____ a.   not tight.
   ____ b.   free.
   ____ c.   careless.

5. | brave | | braved |

   Bruce _____ the danger of the forest.
   From this sentence, you know that
   ____ a.   Bruce went into the forest.
   ____ b.   Bruce was not afraid of the forest.
   ____ c.   Bruce lived near a forest.

Check your answers with the key on page 145.

D   COMPLETING THE SENTENCES

Choose a word from the box that best completes each sentence. Write it on the line.

brave	late	loose	safe	white
or	*or*	*or*	*or*	*or*
braver	later	looser	safer	whiter

1. Estelle is always on time and is never _____.

2. You are _____ in your house than in the street.

3. Larry's shirt is too large and is _____ on him.

4. It was _____ of you to chase the thief.

5. Aaron's _____ car gets dirty quickly.

Check your answers with the key on page 145.

E   USING THE SKILL

Underline the word that best completes each sentence.

1. That banana is much too **ripe riper**.

2. You must be more **gentle gentler** with the dog.

3. The lion's **fierce fiercer** roar hurt my ears.

4. Timothy is **wise wiser** than George.

5. Marion looks **pale paler** today than she did yesterday.

Check your answers with the key on page 145.

F   SUPPLEMENTARY WRITING EXERCISE

The ten new words that were taught in this lesson are:

astonished	beauty	braver	cardboard	cereal
flap	heavens	looser	safer	whiter

Choose any three of your new words from the box and write them in sentences.

1. _____

2. _____

3. _____

Look at the words in the column at the right. Choose the correct word and write it in the blank to best complete the sentence.

Check and Write

1. We watched the dog give _____ to her puppies.

practice   birth   honor

2. Your hands could be a little _____.

cleaner   lower   clearer

3. Janet looks _____ in that big, old chair.

complete   curious   cozy

4. Clark wants to _____ this room into two rooms.

divide   delight   decide

5. This dress was _____ to make.

silent   single   simple

6. I thought you were _____ than that!

smoother   smarter   steeper

7. He is swift to notice danger, and _____ to escape it.

sweeter   stiffer   swifter

8. Turn the light _____ on.

switch   stamp   jar

9. Jonathon was _____ to buy that painting.

testing   pressing   willing

10. Craig's _____ brother just started school.

plainer   younger   scarcer

11. This room is quiet and _____.

cozy   curious   correct

12. Are you _____ to follow Stuart's idea?

winking   weeping   willing

13. I will _____ these cookies among my friends.

decide   divide   discover

14. You have to _____ trains to get to the city.

switch   swift   sweep

15. Your face is much _____ now.

lower   cleaner   looser

16. Jack was happy about the _____ of his daughter.

gift   gaze   birth

17. This puzzle is _____ to do.

single   simple   silent

18. You are looking _____ each time I see you.

younger   thicker   fresher

19. Sometimes I wish I were a lot _____.

smarter   scarcer   smoother

20. This year's planes are _____ than last year's.

sweeter   stiffer   swifter

birth (bėrth), **1.** a coming into life; being born: *the birth of a child.* **2.** a beginning: *the birth of a nation.* **3.** a bringing forth: *the birth of a plan.* **4.** descent; family: *He was a man of humble birth.* *n.*

clean (klēn), **1.** free from dirt or filth; not soiled or stained: *clean clothes. Soap and water make us clean* **2.** having clean habits: *Cats are clean animals.* **3.** make clean: *Washing cleans clothes. Clean up the yard. Clean out your desk.* **4.** do cleaning: *I'm going to clean this morning.* *adj., v., adv.*

di vide (də vīd'), **1.** separate into parts: *A brook divides the field. The river divides and forms two streams.* **2.** separate into equal parts: *When you divide 8 by 2, you get 4.* **3.** to share: *The children divided the candy.* *v.,* **di vid ed, di vid ing,** *n.*

sim ple (sim'pl), **1.** easy to do or understand: *This book is in simple language.* **2.** bare; mere; with nothing added: *My answer is the simple truth.* **3.** plain; without ornament; not rich or showy: *He eats simple food and wears simple clothing.* **4.** common; ordinary: *His parents were simple people.* **5.** dull; weak in mind: *"Simple Simon met a pieman."* *adj.,* **sim pler, sim plest.**

smart (smärt), **1.** feel sharp pain: *His eyes smarted.* **2.** cause sharp pain: *The cut smarts.* **3.** keen; active; lively: *They walked at a smart pace.* **4.** clever; bright: *Jack is a smart boy.* **5.** fresh and neat; in good order: *a smart uniform.* **6.** stylish; fashionable. *v., n., adj., adv.*

switch (swich), **1.** slender stick used in whipping. **2.** whip; strike: *He switched the boys with a birch switch.* **3.** stroke; lash: *The big dog knocked a vase off the table with a switch of his tail.* **4.** move or swing like a switch: *The horse switched his tail.* **5.** device for changing the direction of something, or for making or breaking a connection. A railroad switch shifts a train from one track to another. An electric switch turns the current off or on. **6.** change, turn, or shift by using a switch. **7.** change; turn; shift. *n., v.*

B   USING CONTEXT CLUES

Place an X in front of each correct answer. The word may be used correctly in one or both of the sentences.

1. Where would you find a switch?
   ____ a.   On a wall
   ____ b.   On a lamp

2. Which of the following sentences uses the underlined word correctly?
   ____ a.   Sylvia is a smart dresser.
   ____ b.   We are going to have smart fish for dinner.

3. If Ricky divided his toys among his friends,
   ____ a.   he gave each friend some toys.
   ____ b.   he shared his toys with his friends.

4. If Ernie enjoys simple food the best,
   ____ a.   he likes plain food.
   ____ b.   he is not very smart.

5. Which of the following sentences uses the underlined word correctly?
   ____ a.   With a switch of his tail, the horse ran away.
   ____ b.   Henry switched cars with his wife.

Check your answers with the key on page 145.

C CHECKING THE MEANING

Read the words in the boxes. Choose the word that best completes the sentence under them. Write that word on the line. Then complete the next sentence by placing an X in front of the correct answer.

1. | birth | | births |

   Our cat will soon give _____ to kittens.
   From this sentence, you know that
   ____ a. kittens will soon be born.
   ____ b. kittens are beginning their lives.
   ____ c. our cat is beginning her life.

2. | smart | | smarts |

   The cut on Sandy's arm _____.
   The word you wrote means
   ____ a. lively.
   ____ b. clever.
   ____ c. hurts.

3. | simple | | simplest |

   Marjorie wears the _____ clothes.
   The word you wrote means
   ____ a. oldest.
   ____ b. plainest.
   ____ c. fanciest.

4. | divide | | divided |

   If you _____ ten by two, you will have five.
   The word you wrote means
   ____ a. break one thing into parts.
   ____ b. add parts to make one thing.
   ____ c. to keep for yourself.

5. | clean | | cleaned |

   Our dog is as _____ as our cat.
   The word you wrote means
   ____ a. do cleaning.
   ____ b. not dirty.
   ____ c. make clean.

Check your answers with the key on page 145.

SEQUENCE C-26

D COMPLETING THE SENTENCES

Choose a word from the box that best completes each sentence. Write it on the line.

clean	loud	smart	swift	young
or	*or*	*or*	*or*	*or*
cleaner	louder	smarter	swifter	younger

1. The house is nice and _____.

2. Planes are _____ than trains.

3. I am too _____ to do foolish things.

4. I won't hear you if you don't speak _____.

5. Maurice looks sixteen, but he is _____ than that.

Check your answers with the key on page 145.

E USING THE SKILL

Underline the word that best completes each sentence.

1. That dress is too **tight tighter** for me.
2. The baby's skin is **smooth smoother** than mine.
3. The **neat neater** your work is, the better.
4. It is **cool cooler** today than yesterday.
5. The heat is **great greater** today than yesterday.

Check your answers with the key on page 145.

F SUPPLEMENTARY WRITING EXERCISE

The ten new words that were taught in this lesson are:

birth	cleaner	cozy	divide	simple
smarter	swifter	switch	willing	younger

Choose any three of your new words from the box and write them in sentences.

1. _____
2. _____
3. _____

A LEARNING THE WORDS

Look at the words in the column at the right. Choose the correct word and write it in the blank to best complete the sentence.

Check and Write

1. Murray seems _____ than usual today.

cloudier   puffier   angrier

2. Clean your _____ before you go out.

baggage   bedroom   beehive

3. We are building a _____ fireplace.

bold   brick   chocolate

4. I need to buy some winter _____.

clothing   company   courage

5. The dog's food bowl is _____ than its water bowl.

cheerier   greedier   emptier

6. You need a _____ shirt to wear with that suit.

fancier   dirtier   healthier

7. It is a _____ day today.

foolish   fierce   lovely

8. I must write a _____ to Nancy.

note   nod   net

9. I have never seen a _____ girl.

speedier   prettier   tastier

10. I read that book _____.

twice   safely   softly

11. What did the _____ from Sid say?

leaf   list   note

12. Take Debby into your _____ to play.

treasurer   bedroom   piano

13. The _____ the car, the better I like it.

lazier   lonelier   fancier

14. The baby has grown _____ as tall this year.

course   twice   finally

15. Which picture do you think is _____?

prettier   thirstier   weepier

16. Annie wore a _____ blue dress.

soapy   steamy   lovely

17. All my _____ is too big.

chattering   clothing   fiddling

18. Anything you say will make me _____.

angrier   fancier   lovelier

19. Our new house is made of _____.

wool   straw   brick

20. My closet is _____ than his.

emptier   cloudier   greedier

an gry (ang'grē), 1. feeling or showing anger: *I was very angry when he kicked my dog.* 2. moved by anger: *My friend's angry words hurt my feelings.* 3. stormy. *an angry sky. adj.,* **an gri er, an gri est.**

brick (brik), 1. block of clay baked by sun or fire. Bricks are used to build houses and pave streets. 2. bricks; material bricks are made of. 3. anything shaped like a brick. Ice cream is often sold in bricks. 4. cover with bricks; build or pave with bricks. *n., v.*

emp ty (emp'tē), 1. with nothing in it: *an empty nest.* 2. meaningless; not real: *An empty threat has no force back of it.* 3. pour out or take out all that is in (a thing): *Bill emptied his glass.* 4. flow out: *The Mississippi River empties into the Gulf of Mexico. adj.,* **emp ti er, emp ti est,** *v.,* **emp tied, emp ty ing.**

fan cy (fan'sē), 1. picture to oneself; imagine: *Can you fancy yourself in fairyland?* 2. power to imagine: *Dragons, fairies, and giants in that story are creatures of fancy.* 3. something imagined: *Is it a fancy, or do I hear a sound?* 4. like: *I fancy the idea of having a picnic.* 5. arranged especially to please: *fancy dress, fancy dancing, fancywork. v.,* **fan cied, fan cy ing,** *n., pl.* **fan cies,** *adj.,* **fan ci er, fan ci est.**

note (nōt), 1. a short sentence, phrase, or single word, written down to remind one of what was in a book, a speech, an agreement, etc.: *to take notes of a lecture. I must make a note of that.* 2. a comment, remark, or piece of information added concerning a word or a passage in a book, often to help pupils in studying the book: *Her copy of "Evangeline" has many helpful notes at the back.* 3. very short letter. 4. a written promise to pay a certain amount of money at a certain time. 5. observe; notice; give attention to: *Now note what I do next.* 6. in music, the written sign to show the pitch and the length of a sound. 7. a single musical sound: *Sing this note for me. n., v.,* **not ed, not ing.**

Notes in music:
A, whole note;
B, half note;
C, quarter note;
D, eighth note.

pret ty (prit'ē), 1. pleasing: *a pretty face, a pretty dress, a pretty tune, a pretty story, pretty manners.* Pretty is used to describe people and things that are dainty, sweet, charming, etc., but not stately, grand, elegant, or very important. 2. fairly; rather: *It is pretty late. adj.,* **pret ti er, pret ti est,** *adv.*

B USING CONTEXT CLUES

Place an X in front of each correct answer. The word may be used correctly in one or both of the sentences.

1. Which of the following sentences uses the underlined word correctly?
   _____ a. It is <u>pretty</u> time to go.
   _____ b. Lisa was <u>pretty</u> angry.

2. Where might you find a <u>note</u>?
   _____ a. In a song
   _____ b. At a bank

3. Which of the following sentences uses the underlined word correctly?
   _____ a. Brian <u>fancied</u> himself to be a lover of good music.
   _____ b. What is Howard <u>fancy</u>?

4. Which of the following sentences uses the underlined word correctly?
   _____ a. José <u>bricked</u> the path around the house.
   _____ b. How much did you pay for that <u>brick</u> of ice cream?

5. If Roberta <u>emptied</u> the box of books,
   _____ a. she put the books into the box.
   _____ b. she took the books out of the box.

Check your answers with the key on page 145.

C   CHECKING THE MEANING

Read the words in the boxes. Choose the word that best completes the sentence under them. Write that word on the line. Then complete the next sentence by placing an X in front of the correct answer.

1. | angrier | | angry |

"It is an _____ day today," said Jimmy.
From this sentence, you know that
____ a.   Jimmy is angry.
____ b.   the day is stormy.
____ c.   Jimmy had made someone angry.

2. | note | | noted |

Alicia paid off the _____ in full.
The word you wrote means
____ a.   a short letter.
____ b.   a musical sound.
____ c.   a promise to pay money.

3. | emptied | | empty |

The bathtub _____ in three minutes.
The word you wrote means
____ a.   flowed out.
____ b.   flowed in.
____ c.   followed out.

4. | fancied | | fancy |

Kim _____ the idea of a birthday party for Dawn.
The word you wrote means
____ a.   wanted.
____ b.   liked.
____ c.   planned.

5. | note | | noted |

Betty _____ everything that Marcia did.
The word you wrote means
____ a.   watched.
____ b.   told.
____ c.   sang.

Check your answers with the key on page 145.

D COMPLETING THE SENTENCES

Choose a word from the box that best completes each sentence. Write it on the line.

angry	empty	fancy	happy	pretty
or	*or*	*or*	*or*	*or*
angrier	emptier	fancier	happier	prettier

1. Dad does not _____ cooking outdoors.

2. Sam is _____ about losing his bike.

3. We must _____ the pail before putting it away.

4. The _____ of the two girls won the beauty contest.

5. The _____ Bob is, the more he laughs.

Check your answers with the key on page 145.

E USING THE SKILL

Underline the word that best completes each sentence.

1. Maria's puppy is very **livelier lively**.

2. **Drier Dry** your hands on this rag.

3. This room is much **cozier cozy** since you put in the fireplace.

4. It is **easier easy** to paint a small room than a large one.

5. Your **dirtier dirty** hands must be washed before you eat.

Check your answers with the key on page 145.

F SUPPLEMENTARY WRITING EXERCISE

The ten new words that were taught in this lesson are:

angrier	bedroom	brick	clothing	emptier
fancier	lovely	note	prettier	twice

Choose any three of your new words from the box and write them in sentences.

1. _____

2. _____

3. _____

Look at the words in the column at the right. Choose the correct word and write it in the blank to best complete the sentence.

Check and Write

1. Mr. Arnold is the _____ man I know.

    tightest   cleverest   stiffest

2. His fear of dogs does not make Jeff a _____.

    coconut   chief   coward

3. Vera's _____ dog follows her almost every-where.

    forgotten   pleasant   faithful

4. I could sit and _____ at the fire all night.

    gaze   gnaw   growl

5. It was _____ to get home before dark.

    interesting   impossible   understood

6. I want to _____ about the price of that ring.

    imagine   adventure   inquire

7. I need the _____ piece of ribbon you have.

    narrowest   tenderest   sweetest

8. Ellen is the _____ girl on the team.

    dampest   shortest   clearest

9. Sam's _____ hurts him.

    sore   frown   fur

10. Susan is the _____ person I know.

    faintest   dampest   warmest

11. Edward has been my _____ friend for two years.

    smoothest   plainest   faithful

12. I want only the _____ man for this job.

    flattest   cleverest   deadest

13. The lion in that story is a _____.

    coward   peddler   mayor

14. This is the _____ story I ever read.

    flattest   shortest   narrowest

15. This _____ on my finger is bothering me.

    grain   puff   sore

16. Did you _____ if the job was filled?

    inquire   share   shake

17. This is the _____ road I have ever traveled.

    smartest   freshest   narrowest

18. The kitchen is the _____ room in the house.

    sickest   warmest   calmest

19. It is _____ for me to meet you for lunch.

    impossible   lonely   healthy

20. The boy stopped to _____ at the airplane.

    frown   snap   gaze

clev er (klev'ər), **1.** bright; intelligent; having a ready mind. **2.** skillful in doing some particular thing: *Mr. Jones is a clever carpenter.* **3.** showing skill or intelligence: *a clever trick, a clever answer. adj.*

im pos si ble (im pos'ə bl), **1.** that cannot be or happen: *It is impossible for two and two to make six.* **2.** not possible to use; not to be done: *Few things are impossible.* **3.** not possible to endure: *Tom said a summer without swimming would be impossible. adj.*

nar row (nar'ō), **1.** not wide; having little width: *A path a foot wide is narrow.* **2. Narrows** means a narrow part of a river, strait, sound, valley, pass, etc. **3.** limited; small: *He had only a narrow circle of friends.* **4.** make narrow; become narrow; decrease in width: *The road narrows above the bend.* **5.** close; with a small margin: *He had a narrow escape. adj., n., v.*

short (shôrt), **1.** not long: *a short time, a short life, a short street.* **2.** not tall: *a short man, short grass.* **3.** less than the right amount, measure, standard, etc.: *The cashier is short in his accounts.* **4.** so brief as to be rude: *He was so short with me that I felt hurt.* **5.** suddenly: *He stopped short.* **6.** briefly. **7.** some special meanings are: **cut short,** end suddenly. **fall short, 1.** fail to reach. **2.** be insufficient. **for short,** to make shorter: *Robert was called Rob for short.* **in short,** briefly. **run short, 1.** not have enough. **2.** not be enough. *adj., adv., n.*

sore (sôr), **1.** painful: *The suffering of the poor makes her heart sore.* **2.** causing sorrow: *Their defeat is a sore subject with the members of the team.* **3.** hurt; offended: *He is sore at missing the game.* **4.** painful place on the body where the skin or flesh is broken or bruised. *adj.,* **sor er, sor est,** *n.*

warm (wôrm), **1.** more hot than cold: *Sunshine is warm. The fire made us warm.* **2.** that makes or keeps warm: *We wear warm clothes in winter.* **3.** having or showing lively feelings; zealous; enthusiastic: *a warm welcome, a warm friend, a warm heart. adj., v.*

B   USING CONTEXT CLUES

Place an X in front of each correct answer. The word may be used correctly in one or both of the sentences.

1. If Bill had to cut short his trip,
    ____ a. he was not gone long.
    ____ b. it ended suddenly.

2. Which of the following sentences uses the underlined word correctly?
    ____ a. That big book would not fit on the narrow shelf.
    ____ b. He narrowly missed hitting that car.

3. Which of the following sentences uses the underlined word correctly?
    ____ a. Wendy walked in the warm snow.
    ____ b. Jan greeted us with a warm smile.

4. If Sara ran short of food,
    ____ a. she did not have enough.
    ____ b. she was not tall.

5. If something is impossible,
    ____ a. it cannot happen.
    ____ b. it might happen.

Check your answers with the key on page 146.

| C | CHECKING THE MEANING |

Read the words in the boxes. Choose the word that best completes the sentence under them. Write that word on the line. Then complete the next sentence by placing an X in front of the correct answer.

1. | clever | | cleverest |

   Bruce is very _____ with his hands.
   From this sentence, you know that
   ____ a. Bruce is very smart.
   ____ b. Bruce can make things well.
   ____ c. Bruce is a builder.

2. | short | | shortest |

   Leslie was _____ of money.
   From this sentence, you know that
   ____ a. Leslie did not have enough money.
   ____ b. Leslie was very small.
   ____ c. Leslie left the store suddenly.

3. | warm | | warmest |

   I need a _____ coat for these cold winters.
   The word you wrote means
   ____ a. sunshine and fur.
   ____ b. having a lively feeling.
   ____ c. that which makes or keeps warm.

4. | narrow | | narrows |

   That bottle _____ at the mouth.
   The word you wrote means
   ____ a. gets smaller in width.
   ____ b. is not wide.
   ____ c. is small.

5. | short | | shorter |

   Why was Murray so _____ with Henry?
   From this sentence, you know that
   ____ a. Murray was not as tall as Henry.
   ____ b. Murray did not spend enough time with Henry.
   ____ c. Murray was not polite to Henry.

Check your answers with the key on page 146.

D COMPLETING THE SENTENCES

Choose a word from the box that best completes each sentence. Write it on the line.

clever	narrow	rich	short	warm
or	*or*	*or*	*or*	*or*
cleverest	narrowest	richest	shortest	warmest

1. Are you _____ enough, or shall I turn up the heat?

2. Wendy has earned a lot of money and is very _____.

3. Only the _____ student can win the first prize.

4. Those shoes are too _____ for my wide feet.

5. That is the _____ nap the baby ever took.

Check your answers with the key on page 146.

E USING THE SKILL

Underline the word that best completes each sentence.

1. Marjorie has long, **thick thickest** hair.

2. This is the **steep steepest** hill I ever climbed.

3. Nan's dress was the **plain plainest**.

4. I am the **small smallest** child in my family.

5. There are ten **bright brightest** pennies in my pocket.

Check your answers with the key on page 146.

F SUPPLEMENTARY WRITING EXERCISE

The ten new words that were taught in this lesson are:

| cleverest | coward | faithful | gaze | impossible |
| inquire | narrowest | shortest | sore | warmest |

Choose any three of your new words from the box and write them in sentences.

1. _____

2. _____

3. _____

A LEARNING THE WORDS

Look at the words in the column at the right. Choose the correct word and write it in the blank to best complete the sentence.

Check and Write

1. You must _____ if the price is too high.   reply   complain   prepare

2. I would be _____ with just a short nap.   content   forgotten   faithful

3. What is the _____ time you can get here?   luckiest   earliest   happiest

4. The _____ dog begged for more food.   greedy   wooly   tasty

5. Frank is _____ when he is reading.   dirtiest   happiest   fanciest

6. That was the _____ show I have ever seen.   healthiest   cloudiest   jolliest

7. This has not been my _____ year.   luckiest   greediest   earliest

8. Oscar left this _____ for you.   flame   journey   message

9. Do you _____ this ring?   reward   recognize   receive

10. What is the fastest _____ to the city?   route   root   rack

11. This is the _____ day of my life.   thirstiest   speediest   luckiest

12. Why do you _____ so much?   sting   complain   slide

13. What _____ are you taking on your trip West?   route   inn   journey

14. Will you leave a _____ for Mr. Manfred?   frame   flame   message

15. You may not _____ Malcolm when you see him.   imagine   order   recognize

16. Bruce is quite _____ with his new car.   content   forward   faithful

17. Eileen is the _____ girl I know.   rosiest   earliest   jolliest

18. I spent my _____ days in this house.   sleepiest   happiest   saltiest

19. That _____ man took all my money.   greedy   cheery   stringy

20. What is the _____ train going to the city?   cheeriest   earliest   laziest

com plain (kəm plān'), 1. say something is wrong; find fault. 2. talk about one's pains, troubles, etc. *v.*

con tent (kən tent'), 1. satisfy: *Will it content you if I let you have the candy tomorrow?* 2. satisfied; contented: *Will you be content to wait till tomorrow?* 3. contented state; satisfaction, *v., adj., n.*

greedy (grēd'ē), 1. wanting to get more than one's share. 2. wanting to get a great deal. 3. piggish. *adj.*, **greed i er, greed i est.**

hap py (hap'ē), 1. feeling as you do when you are well and are having a good time; contented. 2. showing that one is glad: *a happy smile, a happy look.* 3. lucky: *By a happy chance I found the watch just where I left it.* 4. fit; successful; fortunate: *a happy way of expressing an idea.* *adj.*, **hap pi er, hap pi est.**

jol ly (jol'ē), 1. merry; full of fun. 2. pleasant. *Used in common talk.* 3. extremely; very. *Used in common talk. adj.,* **jol li er, jol li est,** *adv.*

rec og nize (rek'əg nīz), 1. know again: *You have grown so that I scarcely recognized you.* 2. acknowledge; accept; admit: *I recognize your right to ask that question.* 3. take notice of: *Anyone who wishes to speak in a public meeting should stand up and wait till the chairman recognizes him.* 4. show appreciation of. 5. acknowledge and agree to deal with: *For some years other nations did not recognize the new government. v.,* **rec og nized, rec og niz ing.**

route (rüt or rout), 1. way to go; road: *Will you go to the coast by the northern route?* 2. arrange the way for. 3. send by a certain route. *n., v.,* **rout ed, rout ing.**

B   USING CONTEXT CLUES

Place an X *in front of each correct answer. The word may be used correctly in one or both of the sentences.*

1. If Mr. Johansen <u>complained</u> that his food was cold,
   _____ a.   he always complains about things.
   _____ b.   he was not pleased with his food.

2. If Sylvia won the prize by a <u>happy</u> chance,
   _____ a.   she was healthy.
   _____ b.   she was lucky.

3. Which of the following sentences uses the underlined word correctly?
   _____ a.   Vinny spent the night <u>routing</u> our trip.
   _____ b.   The <u>route</u> of the tree went very deep into the ground.

4. Which of the following sentences uses the underlined word correctly?
   _____ a.   Mickey must be sick if he's <u>content</u> to stay in bed.
   _____ b.   Will you be <u>content</u> if I give you the money tomorrow?

5. Which of the following sentences uses the underlined word correctly?
   _____ a.   The teacher <u>recognized</u> the child who held up his hand.
   _____ b.   I did not <u>recognize</u> Peter.

Check your answers with the key on page 146.

C   CHECKING THE MEANING

Read the words in the boxes. Choose the word that best completes the sentence under them. Write that word on the line. Then complete the next sentence by placing an X in front of the correct answer.

1. | happiest | | happy |

Tony looks _____ today.
The word you wrote means
____ a.   well.
____ b.   glad.
____ c.   greedy.

2. | route | | routed |

Which way does this _____ go?
The word you wrote means
____ a.   road.
____ b.   send.
____ c.   arrange.

3. | jolliest | | jolly |

We all had a _____ good time.
The word you wrote means
____ a.   exciting.
____ b.   silly.
____ c.   very.

4. | greedier | | greedy |

The _____ dog ate all his food.
The word you wrote means
____ a.   piggish.
____ b.   hungry.
____ c.   gray.

5. | complained | | complains |

The woman _____ about how she felt.
From this sentence, you know that
____ a.   the woman did not feel well.
____ b.   the woman talked a lot.
____ c.   the woman had a sore throat.

Check your answers with the key on page 146.

D COMPLETING THE SENTENCES

Choose a word from the box that best completes each sentence. Write it on the line.

early	greedy	happy	jolly	lucky
or	*or*	*or*	*or*	*or*
earliest	greediest	happiest	jolliest	luckiest

1. A _____ clown was full of fun and made us laugh.

2. The winner was _____ enough to guess all the right answers.

3. The _____ we could be there is nine o'clock.

4. Don's bike was found, and he is _____ to have it again.

5. That kitten is the _____ and always wants food.

Check your answers with the key on page 146.

E USING THE SKILL

Underline the word that best completes each sentence.

1. This is the **ugliest ugly** plant I have ever seen.

2. The baby reached for the **shiniest shiny** of the three pennies.

3. Bill is a very **loneliest lonely** man.

4. I feel very **laziest lazy** today.

5. This is the **funniest funny** story I have read in a long time.

Check your answers with the key on page 146.

F SUPPLEMENTARY WRITING EXERCISE

The ten new words that were taught in this lesson are:

complain	content	earliest	greedy	happiest
jolliest	luckiest	message	recognize	route

Choose any three of your new words from the box and write them in sentences.

1. _____

2. _____

3. _____

Look at the words in the column at the right. Choose the correct word and write it in the blank to best complete the sentence.

Check and Write

1. On the _____, I phone Mother once a week.

| average | offer | usual |

2. Jack is the _____ person I know.

| tightest | boldest | dampest |

3. I bought meat at that _____ shop.

| chocolate | canoe | butcher |

4. The old dog's eyes are much _____ today.

| clearer | stiffer | lower |

5. I have to make a _____ of my homework.

| clip | club | copy |

6. Paula is much _____ now.

| friendlier | curlier | cloudier |

7. The children hid in the _____ of the barn.

| lift | loft | leaf |

8. Please _____ that book to me.

| press | prove | pitch |

9. Share your candy, and do not be _____.

| selfish | sleepy | simple |

10. My eyes are the _____ they have ever been.

| freshest | smoothest | sharpest |

11. Ben uses only the _____ colors in his paintings.

| narrowest | boldest | tightest |

12. Your son is taller than _____.

| average | adventure | eighty |

13. I am trying to be _____ with June.

| speedier | thirstier | friendlier |

14. This pencil has the _____ point.

| sharpest | sweetest | sickest |

15. I just bought a _____ of that book.

| frame | copy | form |

16. The _____ woman kept everything for herself.

| polite | police | selfish |

17. The farmer was cleaning the hay _____.

| loft | leak | log |

18. Watch Mitchell _____ the ball!

| pound | patch | pitch |

19. The _____ trimmed the fat from the meat.

| butcher | kangaroo | visitor |

20. The sky is _____ now than it was this morning.

| bolder | steeper | clearer |

bold (bōld), 1. without fear: *The bold boy stood in front of his mother, ready to protect her from danger.* 2. too free in manners: *The bold little boy made faces at us as we passed.* 3. vigorous; free; clear: *The bold outline of the mountain appeared ahead of us.* 4. steep; abrupt: *Bold cliffs overlooked the sea. adj.*

butch er (bùch′ər), 1. man whose work is killing animals for food. 2. man who sells meat. 3. kill (animals) for food. 4. kill (people, animals, etc.) wholesale, needlessly, or cruelly. 5. spoil: *Don't butcher that song! v.*

clear (klir), 1. clean and free from anything that makes it hard to see or understand: *A clear sky is free from clouds. There is a clear view of the sea from that hill. He told a clear story.* 2. make clean and free; get clear: *He will clear the land of trees.* 3. become clear: *It rained and then it cleared.* **Clear up** sometimes means explain: *He cleared up the question of why he had not been there by saying that he had been ill. adj., v., adv.*

copy (kop′ē), 1. thing made to be just like another; thing made on the model of another. A written page, a picture, a dress, or a piece of furniture can be an exact copy of another. 2. make a copy of: *Copy this page. She copied my hat.* 3. be a copy of; be like; imitate. 4. one of a number of books of magazines, of pictures, etc., made at the same printing: *Please get six copies of today's newspaper.* *n., pl.* **cop ies**, *v.*, **cop ied, cop y ing.**

loft (lôft), 1. attic. 2. the room under the roof of a barn: *a hayloft.* 3. a gallery in a church or hall. 4. upper floor of a warehouse or storehouse. *n.*

pitch (pich), 1. throw; fling; hurl; toss: *The men were pitching horseshoes.* 2. in baseball, to throw (a ball) to the man batting. 3. fix firmly in the ground; set up: *to pitch a tent.* 4. fall or plunge forward: *The man lost his balance and pitched down the cliff.* 5. plunge with the bow rising and then falling: *The ship pitched about in the storm.* 6. degree of highness or lowness of a sound. 7. In common talk, **pitch into** means attack and **pitch in** means work vigorously. *v., n.*

sharp (shärp), 1. having a thin cutting edge or a fine point: *a sharp knife, a sharp pin.* 2. having a point; not rounded: *a sharp nose, a sharp corner on a box.* 3. with a sudden change of direction: *a sharp turn.* 4. very cold: *sharp weather, a sharp morning.* 5. severe; biting: *sharp words.* 6. feeling somewhat like a cut or prick; affecting the senses keenly: *a sharp taste, a sharp noise, a sharp pain.* 7. being aware of things quickly: *a sharp eye, sharp ears.* 8. quick in mind; shrewd; clever: *a sharp boy, a sharp lawyer, sharp at a bargain.* 9. promptly; exactly: *Come at one o'clock sharp. adj., adv., n.*

B   USING CONTEXT CLUES

Place an X in front of each correct answer. The word may be used correctly in one or both of the sentences.

1. Which of the following can be pitched?
   ____ a. A tent
   ____ b. A ship

2. Where would you find a loft?
   ____ a. In a church
   ____ b. In the sky

3. If the sky cleared,
   ____ a. there were more clouds.
   ____ b. there were fewer clouds.

4. If Louise butchered the cake she was making,
   ____ a. she killed something.
   ____ b. she spoiled the cake.

5. Which of the following sentences uses the underlined word correctly?
   ____ a. The sharp was swimming near the boat.
   ____ b. I'll meet you at twelve o'clock sharp.

Check your answers with the key on page 146.

C   CHECKING THE MEANING

Read the words in the boxes. Choose the word that best completes the sentence under them. Write that word on the line. Then complete the next sentence by placing an X in front of the correct answer.

1. | pitch | | pitched |

   Let us all _____ in and clean the park.
   From this sentence, you know that
   ____ a.   we will throw something.
   ____ b.   we will fall forward.
   ____ c.   we will work hard.

2. | sharp | | sharpest |

   The dog's _____ ears heard the sound.
   From this sentence, you know that
   ____ a.   the dog could hear very well.
   ____ b.   the dog was clever.
   ____ c.   the sound cut the air.

3. | clear | | cleared |

   The man _____ a patch of land for his garden.
   From this sentence, you know that
   ____ a.   the man saved one piece of land for a garden.
   ____ b.   the man made some land ready for planting.
   ____ c.   the man put a fence around a piece of land.

4. | copied | | copy |

   The boy _____ his sister.
   From this sentence, you know that
   ____ a.   the boy borrowed from his sister.
   ____ b.   the boy tried to be like his sister.
   ____ c.   the boy did not like his sister.

5. | butcher | | butchered |

   The _____ closes his shop every Saturday.
   The word you wrote means
   ____ a.   someone who raises animals.
   ____ b.   someone who sells meat.
   ____ c.   someone who spoils things.

Check your answers with the key on page 146.

D   COMPLETING THE SENTENCES

Choose a word from the box that best completes each sentence. Write it on the line.

bold	clear	friendly	loud	sharp
or	*or*	*or*	*or*	*or*
boldest	clearer	friendlier	loudest	sharpest

1. Don't cut yourself on that _____ knife.

2. The _____ bang could be heard all over the house.

3. Dick is _____ than Janet.

4. The _____ dog walked right into my house.

5. I hope today is _____ than yesterday.

Check your answers with the key on page 146.

E   USING THE SKILL

Underline the word that best completes each sentence.

1. It would be very **nice nicer** to have a picnic.

2. You are quite **healthier healthy**.

3. The **mean meaner** he is, the less I like him.

4. Ida has the **long longest** fingers of anyone I know.

5. This is the **heaviest heavy** of the three bags.

Check your answers with the key on page 146.

F   SUPPLEMENTARY WRITING EXERCISE

The ten new words that were taught in this lesson are:

average	boldest	butcher	clearer	copy
friendlier	loft	pitch	selfish	sharpest

Choose any three of your new words from the box and write them in sentences.

1. _____

2. _____

3. _____

1. If you <u>bend</u> that branch, it may break.
2. I have a <u>bundle</u> of dirty clothes to wash.
3. The <u>eagles</u> are building a new nest.
4. Those <u>flowers</u> grew in my garden.
5. He will <u>gather</u> the fruit and put it in a basket.
6. Do you have any <u>puppets</u> we can use in the show?
7. That seed will soon grow a <u>root</u>.
8. The dog <u>snapped</u> at the rabbit.
9. Our <u>son</u> left his book at school.
10. All the <u>windows</u> of that building are broken.

1. This is one of the <u>beaches</u> that I like.
2. This <u>blanket</u> will keep you warm tonight.
3. How many <u>boxes</u> of Christmas cards did you buy?
4. At the zoo, you can hear the monkeys <u>chatter</u>.
5. The fox <u>crept</u> through the bushes, looking for food.
6. The window was open and the wind made the <u>curtain</u> blow.
7. I did not <u>enjoy</u> that television show.
8. The lake will <u>freeze</u> and then we can skate on it.
9. Air is made of many <u>gases</u>.
10. Nancy had many <u>scratches</u> after a walk in the woods.

G   SENTENCES FOR SPELLING EXERCISE

1. You may have three <u>candies</u> when you have finished your dinner.
2. New York is one of the <u>cities</u> I visit the most.
3. Send this letter first <u>class</u>.
4. There is a <u>crack</u> in the window of the car.
5. Julia <u>finally</u> heard from her sister after six years.
6. When you take off your clothes, you should <u>hang</u> them up.
7. When this building is finished, there will be five <u>libraries</u> in town.
8. Have you named all the <u>puppies</u>?
9. I <u>replied</u> to your letter as soon as I got it.
10. There are <u>thirty</u> steps to climb when you come to my house.

G   SENTENCES FOR SPELLING EXERCISE

1. When you finish feeding the <u>calves</u>, feed the pigs.
2. The teacher was sitting at his <u>desk</u>.
3. Leave your wet shoes in the <u>hall</u>.
4. Put the milk in this <u>jar</u>.
5. How do you like your <u>job</u>?
6. Did you wear both these <u>scarves</u> today?
7. Put these dishes on those <u>shelves</u> in the kitchen.
8. Look at all those cracks in the <u>sidewalk</u>!
9. I have a very <u>special</u> surprise for you today.
10. "Most of these men are <u>thieves</u>," said the policeman.

1. I'll wait for you by the <u>bench</u> in the park.
2. Let's ride our <u>bicycles</u> to the store.
3. The snow looks beautiful on the <u>branches</u> of that tree.
4. There's a <u>chance</u> that you might lose your job.
5. Matt Fisk will <u>coach</u> the football team this year.
6. How many <u>halves</u> are there in eight?
7. One of these <u>ladies</u> will win a trip to New York.
8. Did you <u>lose</u> the book you took from the library?
9. Our <u>team</u> of horses might just win the race!
10. I try not to <u>worry</u> about Sam, but I alway do.

1. Why <u>can't</u> you come to the party?
2. You should <u>chew</u> your food carefully.
3. I hope Mario wins the 100-yard <u>dash</u>.
4. Laura <u>doesn't</u> like that kind of food.
5. Mitchell <u>isn't</u> here today.
6. Do you think Bruce <u>meant</u> what he said?
7. Are we having <u>meat</u> tonight?
8. Jack wants to get <u>rid</u> of these pictures.
9. Did the milk <u>spoil?</u>
10. Why <u>won't</u> you join us on our trip?

G SENTENCES FOR SPELLING EXERCISE

1. When Chuck arrives, we can all go to the park.
2. Michele continues to see Fred every day after work.
3. When Phyllis dreams she sometimes laughs in her sleep.
4. My dog has brown fur with white spots.
5. The library is about a mile down this street.
6. For a moment, I thought you were my friend Seth.
7. "You must follow every rule if you want to be on my team," said the boy.
8. Take your time and don't rush with your work.
9. The girls were skating on the sidewalk.
10. When Frank signals you, run for the house as fast as you can.

G SENTENCES FOR SPELLING EXERCISE

1. The little boy has already broken his new toy.
2. Mary left her boots at school.
3. Clean your brushes when you are finished painting.
4. The children are playing in a cave near our house.
5. The baby was eager to have some milk.
6. It doesn't matter what time you come.
7. Nancy always mixes all her food together.
8. I want to pack away these winter clothes.
9. Scott searches for his lost dog every day.
10. The park stretches out for many miles.

1. We will be moving next <u>autumn</u>.

2. The lives of many animals are in <u>danger</u>.

3. Matt has <u>decided</u> to leave his job.

4. There is always a lot of <u>excitement</u> when you move to a new house.

5. Herb's father gave him a <u>gun</u> for his birthday.

6. The mother only <u>imagined</u> that her baby was crying.

7. Joannie <u>invited</u> me to help her paint her room.

8. Billy weighs <u>less</u> than Murray.

9. Alice <u>practiced</u> tying her shoes.

10. That was Sid's best <u>shot</u> with his new gun.

1. I am alway <u>awake</u> by eight o'clock.

2. You <u>disappeared</u> before I could ask my question.

3. Chuck <u>explained</u> how to get to his house.

4. Don't <u>forget</u> to lock the door when you leave.

5. David <u>forgot</u> to do his homework.

6. Wendy <u>learned</u> about the Indians in school today.

7. Did you <u>lose</u> your book?

8. I <u>promise</u> to meet you at nine o'clock.

9. Annie <u>screamed</u> because she was afraid.

10. I read <u>twenty</u> pages of my book last night.

G   SENTENCES FOR SPELLING EXERCISE

1. The <u>army</u> marched through the streets of the city.
2. When did that great <u>discovery</u> take place?
3. The rainy day just <u>dragged</u>.
4. It is an <u>honor</u> for us to have you visit our house.
5. What <u>language</u> do you speak?
6. A silver <u>medal</u> goes to the second place winner.
7. Nancy <u>skipped</u> making her bed this morning.
8. The men <u>trotted</u> around the field.
9. Linda is very <u>wrapped</u> up in her troubles.
10. Have you <u>written</u> to your sister?

G   SENTENCES FOR SPELLING EXERCISE

1. Have you ever been <u>aboard</u> an airplane?
2. The <u>American</u> flag is red, white, and blue.
3. Does Philip <u>appear</u> to be taller than Jim?
4. I watched Jane and Jim <u>carve</u> their names in a tree.
5. Everyone <u>cheered</u> when Matt won the race.
6. While Marcia <u>chopped</u> the eggs, Will buttered the bread.
7. Frank <u>earns</u> more money than Sam.
8. My puppy has <u>grown</u> since we got him.
9. I sometimes <u>save</u> time by running home.
10. The room <u>sparkled</u> after I cleaned it.

| G | SENTENCES FOR SPELLING EXERCISE |

1. I keep all my books in a box in my <u>bedroom</u>.
2. When my clothes <u>dried</u>, I hung them in the closet.
3. I like the <u>glitter</u> of a clean kitchen.
4. It's not nice to <u>grab</u> the biggest piece of pie.
5. Little Jacob always gets <u>lively</u> when it's time to go to bed.
6. Laura said she would never get <u>married</u>.
7. I am not <u>satisfied</u> with just a piece of fruit for lunch.
8. Mice are <u>studied</u> by doctors.
9. A <u>sudden</u> change in the weather can give you a cold.
10. If <u>you're</u> very rich you do not have to work.

| G | SENTENCES FOR SPELLING EXERCISE |

1. I feel <u>awful</u> today.
2. The sun has <u>begun</u> to set.
3. There was a <u>blinding</u> snow storm yesterday.
4. My friends and I always <u>exercise</u> together.
5. Lisa is <u>expecting</u> a letter today.
6. A <u>group</u> of us are going to the show.
7. Timothy kept <u>hammering</u> until he finished what he was making.
8. We can use this <u>hollow</u> bowl to hold our money.
9. Jim is <u>known</u> as a smart boy.
10. Phyllis is <u>spraying</u> water on the leaves of her plants.

G SENTENCES FOR SPELLING EXERCISE

1. They will soon be <u>announcing</u> the start of the ball game.
2. The <u>ashes</u> from the fire are cool now.
3. I was <u>certain</u> you would be at home.
4. I am looking for a car that won't <u>cost</u> much money.
5. A strong wind is <u>forcing</u> the trees to bend.
6. Which American <u>hero</u> do you like best?
7. Selma is the <u>president</u> of our club.
8. Many men and women are <u>rescuing</u> the people hurt in the crash.
9. Come home quickly without making a <u>scene</u>.
10. Some people are always <u>struggling</u> to earn money.

G SENTENCES FOR SPELLING EXERCISE

1. I want to <u>arrange</u> for a housekeeper.
2. These old clothes will be a <u>blessing</u> to those people.
3. There was a <u>clapping</u> noise, and then all was quiet.
4. The <u>date</u> of America's birthday is July 4.
5. Amanda was <u>dripping</u> wet after walking in the rain.
6. We have <u>forgotten</u> to put gas in the car.
7. The baby likes <u>hugging</u> his teddy bear when he goes to sleep.
8. We stay home and read the <u>newspaper</u> every Sunday.
9. Watch the skater <u>spinning</u> on the ice!
10. It takes a lot of <u>wisdom</u> to understand people.

G SENTENCES FOR SPELLING EXERCISE

1. The <u>bloody</u> war finally ended.
2. In the summer I like to hang the wash <u>outdoors</u>.
3. I did my <u>share</u> of the work.
4. Brian is being very <u>silent</u> about where he was.
5. Why are you so <u>sleepy</u> today?
6. There was a <u>tap</u> at my front door.
7. Water is the best drink when you are <u>thirsty</u>.
8. These new gloves keep my hands <u>toasty</u>.
9. I am expecting a <u>visitor</u> tonight.
10. Did you know that a <u>woodpecker</u> eats insects?

G SENTENCES FOR SPELLING EXERCISE

1. If you will <u>amuse</u> the baby, I'll be able to make dinner.
2. By <u>borrowing</u> clothes from my brother, I can save money.
3. Can both men and women enter this <u>contest</u>?
4. Julio's parents will <u>crown</u> his hard work by getting him a bicycle.
5. Roger wants to <u>grease</u> his car.
6. Carol is a very <u>healthy</u> girl.
7. The baby kept <u>refusing</u> to eat.
8. Good ice cream is very <u>scarce</u>.
9. Pedro used to be <u>stout</u>, but he lost a lot of weight.
10. Mr. Paco was <u>worried</u> because he lost his money.

G   SENTENCES FOR SPELLING EXERCISE

1. There was a blast from the ship's horn.
2. Always stay calm when you drive.
3. What, exactly, do you want?
4. If you speak politely, people will probably listen.
5. Drive safely.
6. Ann was serious when she said she would not go.
7. The lion silently attacked the animal.
8. Fred walks softly in his new shoes.
9. Josh was startled out of a deep sleep.
10. I don't like Peter to ride his bike in traffic.

G   SENTENCES FOR SPELLING EXERCISE

1. No one was hurt in the automobile crash.
2. Don't believe everything a boaster says.
3. I don't know how my watch broke.
4. I would like to be the discoverer of new lands.
5. An enjoyer of good food will sometimes get fat.
6. A smile always looks better than a frown.
7. Jess's sadness was hidden by a smile.
8. The police caught the thief in just four days.
9. The robber went into the house through the window.
10. The speaker asked everyone to be quiet.

G SENTENCES FOR SPELLING EXERCISE

1. My children always behave very well.
2. That is not a good example of what I want.
3. The knight was brave and daring.
4. Irv will rebuild the barn next week.
5. I don't think Sean will remarry.
6. I had to reread that sentence three times.
7. Can you restate what you just read?
8. Dad will squeeze those oranges.
9. We leave food outside for stray animals.
10. If Helen would keep her temper, she would have less trouble.

G SENTENCES FOR SPELLING EXERCISE

1. Cliff's answer was correct.
2. Babies are curious about everything.
3. The deaf woman sat by the window.
4. That was a dumb thing to do.
5. I have a lot of clothes to press.
6. After running, my heart beats rapidly.
7. Marilyn looks uncomfortable sitting in that small chair.
8. If you uncover its roots, the plant will die.
9. In one unguarded minute, Barbara's baby wandered off.
10. Adam likes to read unusual books.

G SENTENCES FOR SPELLING EXERCISE

1. The number of people in the stores today would <u>amaze</u> you.
2. I don't like the way Chico looks with a <u>beard</u>.
3. I am <u>breathless</u> because I have been running.
4. Mark's <u>camera</u> broke, so he couldn't take any pictures.
5. I always keep my good <u>jewelry</u> in a safe place.
6. Albert gave Doris a silver <u>necklace</u>.
7. There is no <u>paste</u> on the back of this stamp.
8. Bobby was upset by some <u>senseless</u> thing that James said.
9. The little boy's <u>spotless</u> clothes were soon full of mud.
10. That oil painting is far from <u>worthless</u>!

G SENTENCES FOR SPELLING EXERCISE

1. I can give you a <u>bargain</u> on that table.
2. This suit was very <u>costly</u>.
3. Eric did not <u>deserve</u> the marks he got in school.
4. The <u>drifter</u> got a part-time job to earn some money.
5. It costs a <u>fortune</u> to travel these days.
6. The elephants' <u>keeper</u> is a strong man.
7. Paddy dropped the <u>pitcher</u> of milk.
8. I want to <u>replace</u> the book I lost.
9. The Christmas <u>season</u> will soon be here.
10. Jennifer left her ironing <u>undone</u>.

1. You will be <u>astonished</u> by what I have to tell you.
2. Your daughter is a <u>beauty</u>!
3. Winning a fight does not show that you are <u>braver</u> than Shep.
4. Use this <u>cardboard</u> for your sign.
5. Hot <u>cereal</u> is a good breakfast food.
6. Close the box <u>flap</u> to keep the cookies fresh.
7. The sun is high in the <u>heavens</u> at this time of day.
8. My new shoes are <u>looser</u> than my old ones.
9. Baseball is <u>safer</u> than football.
10. I wish my teeth were <u>whiter</u>.

1. Meredith just gave <u>birth</u> to a girl.
2. You used to keep your room much <u>cleaner</u>.
3. It is so <u>cozy</u> sitting by the fire.
4. Norma tried to <u>divide</u> the pie into ten pieces.
5. Jay's homework was so <u>simple</u>, he finished in ten minutes.
6. Children seem to be <u>smarter</u> than ever these days.
7. You'll have to run <u>swifter</u> than Tom if you hope to win the race.
8. Please <u>switch</u> the station on the radio.
9. I am ready, <u>willing</u>, and able to do the job.
10. Who is <u>younger</u>, you or your sister?

G SENTENCES FOR SPELLING EXERCISE

1. You make me angrier with every word you say.
2. There is a closet in each bedroom of this house.
3. We are putting up a brick wall in our kitchen.
4. Is that all the summer clothing you have?
5. This room would look emptier if this table were in that corner.
6. Judy likes fancier things than I do.
7. It was lovely to see Elaine after so many years.
8. Send Harriet a thank-you note for the gift.
9. You look prettier with your hair short.
10. I need a piece of paper twice as large as this one.

G SENTENCES FOR SPELLING EXERCISE

1. Tracy is the cleverest girl I know.
2. The coward ran and hid behind a car.
3. Do you have a faithful dog?
4. I like to sit at the beach and gaze into the water.
5. Do you still believe space travel is impossible?
6. John called to inquire about Nick.
7. Get me the narrowest piece of wood you can find.
8. Today is the shortest day of the year.
9. My throat is sore.
10. Put on your warmest coat.

G   SENTENCES FOR SPELLING EXERCISE

1. Elliot doesn't ever complain about the food he eats.
2. Would you be content to stay at home tonight?
3. I will get there at the earliest time possible.
4. That greedy man would not part with his money.
5. I am happiest with a few friends around me.
6. We had the jolliest time at Steven's party!
7. Judy is the luckiest woman here.
8. "Did my wife leave a message?" asked Mr. Townsend.
9. I did not recognize Ed.
10. This is the shortest route to Mary's house.

G   SENTENCES FOR SPELLING EXERCISE

1. Your work must be better than average if you want to be a doctor.
2. Draw the boldest line you can.
3. That butcher sells only fresh meat.
4. The road was clearer after the fog disappeared.
5. Don't copy your friend's work.
6. I wonder why Joan is friendlier than usual.
7. We store many old things in our loft.
8. Mickey will pitch in today's baseball game.
9. The selfish dog wouldn't let the puppy near his food.
10. Philip was the sharpest boy in his class.

ANSWER KEY

Sequences C-1 — C-3

SEQUENCE 1	SEQUENCE 2	SEQUENCE 3

SEQUENCE 1

B (page 2)

1. a, b
2. a, b
3. a, b
4. a, b
5. b

C (page 3)

1. bundled, c
2. gather, a
3. rooting, a
4. snapped, b
5. son, b

D (page 4)

1. flowers
2. roots
3. puppet
4. windows
5. eagles

E (page 4)

1. television
2. minutes
3. waves
4. question
5. dollars

SEQUENCE 2

B (page 6)

1. a, b
2. a
3. b
4. a
5. a, b

C (page 7)

1. scratches, b
2. creeping, c
3. chatter, b
4. blanket, a
5. froze, b

D (page 8)

1. scratch
2. box
3. curtains
4. gas
5. beaches

E (page 8)

1. dresses
2. bush
3. glasses
4. guesses
5. cross

SEQUENCE 3

B (page 10)

1. a
2. a
3. a, b
4. a, b
5. b

C (page 11)

1. class, c
2. crack, b
3. hang, c
4. cracked, a
5. library, b

D (page 12)

1. candy
2. library
3. puppies
4. classes
5. cities

E (page 12)

1. story
2. baby
3. families
4. country
5. pennies

ANSWER KEY

Sequences C-4 — C-6

SEQUENCE 4

B (page 14)

1. b
2. a, b
3. a
4. a, b
5. a, b

C (page 15)

1. calves, b
2. special, b
3. scarves, a
4. hall, c
5. jarred, a

D (page 16)

1. sidewalk
2. thief
3. calves
4. shelves
5. scarf

E (page 16)

1. hooves
2. elf
3. leaves
4. yourself
5. wolves

SEQUENCE 5

B (page 18)

1. a, b
2. a, b
3. a, b
4. a
5. b

C (page 19)

1. worried, c
2. chance, b
3. coach, c
4. lost, a
5. branches, c

D (page 20)

1. worry
2. branches
3. half
4. bicycle
5. lady

E (page 20)

1. ponies
2. dishes
3. fights
4. scarf
5. party

SEQUENCE 6

B (page 22)

1. a
2. b
3. a, b
4. a, b
5. a

C (page 23)

1. rid, b
2. dashed, a
3. means, a
4. spoil, c
5. chewed, b

D (page 24)

1. doesn't
2. will
3. wouldn't
4. can't *or* won't
5. isn't

E (page 24)

1. couldn't
2. haven't
3. don't
4. was
5. didn't

SEQUENCE 7	**SEQUENCE 8**	**SEQUENCE 9**
B (page 26)	**B** (page 30)	**B** (page 34)
1. a, b	1. b	1. a
2. a, b	2. b	2. a, b
3. a	3. a	3. a
4. a, b	4. a	4. a, b
5. b	5. **a**	5. a
C (page 27)	**C** (page 31)	**C** (page 35)
1. rushed, c	1. brush, b	1. practice, b
2. mile, a	2. mixes, a	2. shots, b
3. continue, a	3. searching, b	3. imagined, c
4. dreams, a	4. packs, c	4. inviting, a
5. moment, b	5. stretched, a	5. decide, a
D (page 28)	**D** (page 32)	**D** (page 36)
1. dream	1. stretch	1. imagine
2. arrive	2. watches	2. invite
3. signal	3. mix	3. faced
4. laughs	4. search	4. practiced
5. continue	5. brushes	5. decided
E (page 28)	**E** (page 32)	**E** (page 36)
1. write	1. wish	1. excited
2. skate	2. teach	2. joking
3. leaves	3. catches	3. pleased
4. visit	4. fixes	4. timed
5. follows	5. guess	5. whistled

ANSWER KEY

Sequences C-10 — C-12

SEQUENCE 10

B (page 38)

1. b
2. a, b
3. b
4. b
5. a, b

C (page 39)

1. disappeared, a
2. forgot, c
3. screamed, c
4. promise, a
5. learn, b

D (page 40)

1. learn
2. opened
3. disappeared
4. explain
5. screamed

E (page 40)

1. answered
2. wondered
3. shout
4. pointed
5. hunted

SEQUENCE 11

B (page 42)

1. b
2. b
3. a, b
4. b
5. a, b

C (page 43)

1. army, a
2. trotting, c
3. skipped, c
4. wrap, b
5. dragged, c

D (page 44)

1. skip
2. slipped
3. wrap
4. trot
5. dragged

E (page 44)

1. plan
2. begged
3. stir
4. nodded
5. drummed

SEQUENCE 12

B (page 46)

1. a
2. a, b
3. b
4. b
5. b

C (page 47)

1. American, b
2. earn, c
3. cheer, a
4. appeared, a
5. save, b

D (page 48)

1. carve
2. sparkled
3. earn
4. cheered
5. chopped

E (page 48)

1. repeats
2. crashes
3. manage
4. circling
5. pinned

ANSWER KEY

Sequences C-13 — C-15

SEQUENCE 13

B (page 50)

1. a
2. b
3. a
4. a
5. a

C (page 51)

1. dry, c
2. grabbed, b
3. studied, a
4. satisfy, a
5. studies, c

D (page 52)

1. satisfied
2. married
3. cry
4. dry
5. studied

E (page 52)

1. carry
2. reply
3. emptied
4. readied
5. hurry

SEQUENCE 14

B (page 54)

1. a
2. b
3. a, b
4. b
5. a

C (page 55)

1. group, a
2. hammered, b
3. blind, b
4. begun, c
5. exercising, a

D (page 56)

1. expecting
2. blinding
3. spray
4. hammer
5. storm

E (page 56)

1. disappointing
2. attacked
3. ironing
4. pretending
5. sails

SEQUENCE 15

B (page 58)

1. a
2. a
3. b
4. b
5. a

C (page 59)

1. scene, b
2. certain, c
3. forced, a
4. cost, b
5. struggle, a

D (page 60)

1. announce
2. struggling
3. scare
4. force
5. rescue

E (page 60)

1. shaking
2. escaped
3. rattle
4. smoke
5. daring

ANSWER KEY

Sequences C-16 — C-18

SEQUENCE 16	SEQUENCE 17	SEQUENCE 18

SEQUENCE 16

B (page 62)

1. a, b
2. b
3. a
4. a, b
5. b

C (page 63)

1. blessing, a
2. arranged, c
3. dated, b
4. spinning, b
5. hugging, c

D (page 64)

1. skipping
2. clap
3. hug
4. drip
5. spinning

E (page 64)

1. slapped
2. tip
3. wrapped
4. dragging
5. drumming

SEQUENCE 17

B (page 66)

1. a
2. a, b
3. a, b
4. a
5. a, b

C (page 67)

1. silent, b
2. shared, c
3. toast, b
4. tapped, a
5. bloody, b

D (page 68)

1. luck
2. sleep
3. bloody
4. toast
5. thirsty

E (page 68)

1. steam
2. bushy
3. wool
4. oil
5. rain

SEQUENCE 18

B (page 70)

1. a
2. a
3. a
4. b
5. b

C (page 71)

1. crown, c
2. scarce, b
3. worried, a
4. crown, b
5. contesting, a

D (page 72)

1. borrow
2. amusing
3. worried
4. refuse
5. health

E (page 72)

1. tried
2. floating
3. nibbled
4. tooting
5. creamy

ANSWER KEY

Sequences C-19 — C-21

SEQUENCE 19	SEQUENCE 20	SEQUENCE 21

SEQUENCE 19

B (page 74)

1. a
2. a
3. a, b
4. b
5. a, b

C (page 75)

1. soft, c
2. seriously, c
3. blast, a
4. calm, a
5. traffic, c

D (page 76)

1. softly
2. politely
3. exactly
4. silent
5. calm

E (page 76)

1. certain
2. usually
3. quickly
4. proud
5. sick

SEQUENCE 20

B (page 78)

1. b
2. a
3. b
4. a, b
5. a

C (page 79)

1. boast, b
2. policing, c
3. spoke, b
4. break, b
5. broke, a

D (page 80)

1. enjoy
2. robber
3. speaker
4. discover
5. boast

E (page 80)

1. wanderer
2. print
3. sweep
4. bowler
5. sing

SEQUENCE 21

B (page 82)

1. a, b
2. a
3. a
4. a, b
5. a, b

C (page 83)

1. reading, b
2. stray, a
3. temper, a
4. example, c
5. squeezed, a

D (page 84)

1. build
2. wrap
3. remarry
4. reread
5. restate

E (page 84)

1. redo
2. make
3. reload
4. store
5. finish

SEQUENCE 22	**SEQUENCE 23**	**SEQUENCE 24**
B (page 86)	**B** (page 90)	**B** (page 94)
1. a	1. a	1. a, b
2. a, b	2. a	2. a, b
3. b	3. a, b	3. b
4. a, b	4. a, b	4. a
5. b	5. a	5. a
C (page 87)	**C** (page 91)	**C** (page 95)
1. curious, c	1. beard, c	1. costly, a
2. rapids, c	2. breathless, b	2. bargained, c
3. pressed, b	3. paste, b	3. seasoning, a
4. unusual, a	4. necklace, b	4. drifted, b
5. press, b	5. senseless, a	5. pitcher, b
D (page 88)	**D** (page 92)	**D** (page 96)
1. unusual	1. worth	1. place
2. comfortable	2. beard	2. done
3. noticed	3. senseless	3. drift
4. guarded	4. breathless	4. cost
5. cover	5. spot	5. pitcher
E (page 88)	**E** (page 92)	**E** (page 96)
1. unable	1. careless	1. correctly
2. welcome	2. star	2. diver
3. Untie	3. tire	3. paint
4. sure	4. priceless	4. spoiled
5. unprepared	5. toothless	5. joy

144

ANSWER KEY

Sequences C-25 — C-27

SEQUENCE C-25	SEQUENCE C-26	SEQUENCE C-27

SEQUENCE C-25

B (page 98)

1. b
2. b
3. b
4. a
5. a, b

C (page 99)

1. safe, b
2. beauty, a
3. flapped, b
4. loose, b
5. braved, a

D (page 100)

1. late
2. safer
3. loose
4. brave
5. white

E (page 100)

1. ripe
2. gentle
3. fierce
4. wiser
5. paler

SEQUENCE C-26

B (page 102)

1. a, b
2. a
3. a, b
4. a
5. a, b

C (page 103)

1. birth, a
2. smarts, c
3. simplest, b
4. divide, a
5. clean, b

D (page 104)

1. clean
2. swifter
3. smart
4. louder
5. younger

E (page 104)

1. tight
2. smoother
3. neater
4. cooler
5. greater

SEQUENCE C-27

B (page 106)

1. b
2. a, b
3. a
4. a, b
5. b

C (page 107)

1. angry, b
2. note, c
3. emptied, a
4. fancied, b
5. noted, a

D (page 108)

1. fancy
2. angry
3. empty
4. prettier
5. happier

E (page 108)

1. lively
2. Dry
3. cozier
4. easier
5. dirty

ANSWER KEY

Sequences C-28 — C-30

SEQUENCE 28	SEQUENCE 29	SEQUENCE 30
B (page 110)	**B** (page 114)	**B** (page 118)
1. b	1. b	1. a, b
2. a, b	2. b	2. a
3. b	3. a	3. b
4. a	4. a, b	4. b
5. a	5. a, b	5. b
C (page 111)	**C** (page 115)	**C** (page 119)
1. clever, b	1. happy, b	1. pitch, c
2. short, a	2. route, a	2. sharp, a
3. warm, c	3. jolly, c	3. cleared, b
4. narrows, a	4. greedy, a	4. copied, b
5. short, c	5. complained, a	5. butcher, b
D (page 112)	**D** (page 116)	**D** (page 120)
1. warm	1. jolly	1. sharp
2. rich	2. lucky	2. loud
3. cleverest	3. earliest	3. friendlier
4. narrow	4. happy	4. bold
5. shortest	5. greediest	5. clearer
E (page 112)	**E** (page 116)	**E** (page 120)
1. thick	1. ugliest	1. nice
2. steepest	2. shiniest	2. healthy
3. plainest	3. lonely	3. meaner
4. smallest	4. lazy	4. longest
5. bright	5. funniest	5. heaviest

PROGRESS CHART

SCORE 20 POINTS FOR EACH CORRECT ANSWER IN EXERCISES D AND E.
SCORE 10 POINTS FOR EACH CORRECT ANSWER IN EXERCISE G.

(EXAMPLE)

SEQUENCE NUMBER	SEQUENCE SECTION SCORE			PAGE NUMBER	DATE
	D	E	G		
C-1	80			4	September 12, 1989
		100		4	September 12, 1989
			90		September 15, 1989

SEQUENCE NUMBER	SEQUENCE SECTION SCORE			PAGE NUMBER	DATE
	D	E	G		
C-1					
C-2					
C-3					

SEQUENCE NUMBER	SEQUENCE SECTION SCORE			PAGE NUMBER	DATE
	D	E	G		
C-4					
C-5					
C-6					
C-7					
C-8					
C-9					
C-10					
C-11					

SEQUENCE NUMBER	SEQUENCE SECTION SCORE			PAGE NUMBER	DATE
	D	E	G		
C-12					
C-13					
C-14					
C-15					
C-16					
C-17					
C-18					
C-19					

SEQUENCE NUMBER	SEQUENCE SECTION SCORE			PAGE NUMBER	DATE
	D	E	G		
C-20					
C-21					
C-22					
C-23					
C-24					
C-25					
C-26					
C-27					

SEQUENCE NUMBER	SEQUENCE SECTION SCORE			PAGE NUMBER	DATE
	D	E	G		
C-28					
C-29					
C-30					